DARK FUTURES

WHEN THE LIGHTS

GO DOWN

Also by Nick Dunn:

Dark Matters: A Manifesto for the Nocturnal City

Co-edited with Tim Edensor:

Rethinking Darkness: Cultures, Histories, Practices

Dark Skies: Places, Practices, Communities

DARK FUTURES

WHEN THE LIGHTS

GO DOWN

Nick Dunn

zer0
books

London, UK
Washington, DC, USA

CollectiveInk

First published by Zer0 Books, 2025
Zer0 Books is an imprint of Collective Ink Ltd.,
Unit 11, Shepperton House, 89 Shepperton Road, London, N1 3DF
office@collectiveinkbooks.com
www.collectiveinkbooks.com
www.zero-books.net

For distributor details and how to order, please visit the 'Ordering' section
on our website.

Text copyright: Nick Dunn, 2024

Paperback ISBN: 978 1 78904 361 7
eBook ISBN: 978 1 78904 362 4
PCN: 2024942557

A CIP catalogue record for this book is available from the British Library.

Design credit(s): Lapiz Digital

UK: Printed and bound by CPI Group (UK) Ltd, Croydon, CR0 4YY
Printed in North America by CPI GPS partners

We operate a distinctive and ethical publishing philosophy in
all areas of our business, from our global network of authors to
production and worldwide distribution.

For Evelyn

amplecti tenebras

In memory of Jen

ad astra

Nick Dunn is a writer, educator, and performer. He is Executive Director of Imagination, the design and architecture research lab at Lancaster University, where he is also Professor of Urban Design. Nick is the founding Director of the Dark Design Lab, examining the impacts of nocturnal urban activity on people, planet, and the many species we share it with. He is also a Director for DarkSky UK, working to protect dark skies for the benefit of future generations. Nick is the author of *Dark Matters* (2016) and co-editor of *Rethinking Darkness* (2020) and *Dark Skies* (2023). Born in Salford, he lives in Manchester. He regularly nightwalks across both cities and beyond.

CONTENTS

ACKNOWLEDGEMENTS

Many of the ideas in *Dark Futures* were initially rehearsed as talks, walks, and conversations. I am grateful to the audiences, wayfarers, and raconteurs that listened and shared their thoughts and gave me encouragement and feedback along the way. The reception for my previous book, *Dark Matters*, provided enough positive energy to motivate this work, which forms a sort of sequel in that several of the ideas for the book you are currently reading originated at the time of writing the former. It is also true that these seeds needed time to bloom in the shadows, away from the scrutiny of light for a while. Much like the dark matter that constitutes about six times what is visible in the universe, there is much that has happened around the writing of this book that shaped it.

First and foremost, I would like to thank my daughter Evelyn, whose boundless imagination and creativity is a daily and nightly reminder of the wonders of being alive. Next, I would like to thank Angela, Kirsty, and Sarah for being bright stars in the constellation of life. Enormous thanks also to Paul Burgess and Rob Baillie, whose friendship and sharing of time, stories, music, and humour are greatly appreciated. Although this book navigates its way across an array of issues concerning ideologies, ecologies, and technologies, and is therefore deliberate in its attempt to offer a wide field of vision in its approach, many of its ideas and the thinking around them were walked through in nocturnal and diurnal landscapes of Manchester. For this, I have huge gratitude to my walking companions Zola and Camion, angular and avuncular guides to the multisensory experience of places. I have continued to find nightwalking essential to making sense of a complex world, living proof that amongst the darkness there is always meaning.

My colleagues at the Dark Design Lab, Rupert Griffiths and Élisabeth de Bézenac, continue to provide inspiration and excellent company through their work into nocturnal rhythms and urban nights, respectively. I would also like to thank the wider Imagination team at Lancaster University for being a community of brilliant people doing wonderful things for the benefit of people, place, and planet. In addition, I would like to thank Simon Buckley, aka Not Quite Light, for our ruminations and journeying into the dark. Tim Edensor for his generosity and enthusiasm for engaging with darkness in its many forms. Kaisu Koski, whose work on multispecies relationships and the climate crisis has been motivating. Roy Alexander and the fellow directors of DarkSky UK, indefatigable defenders of dark skies. Friso Wiersum, Nikos Doulos, and Bart Witte (aka Expodium) for their ongoing friendship and forays into the night that continue to energise. Taylor Stone for our ongoing exchanges about dark design and the idea of darkening cities that is very much rooted in his work. Derek Pardue for our continuing meditations on dusk. Manuel Garcia-Ruiz and Jordi Nofre for their organisation and social skills in bringing together and sustaining a vibrant global community of researchers working across the different dimensions of night studies through their leadership of the annual International Conference on Night Studies. Beyond these friends and collaborators, it has been a genuine pleasure to meet people from many different corners of the world who share an interest in darkness, and the community of academics and creative practitioners that dwell in the shadowlands, urban or otherwise, have proved inspirational. These generous encounters have enabled me to learn how significant the subject of darkness truly is, cutting across time and space, culture and history, theory and practice in spectacular and often surprising ways.

Finally, I would like to give my considerable thanks to the good people at Zer0 Books, whose openness and generosity towards this title was much appreciated. There is much to share in the pages that follow. So without further delay, let us explore *Dark Futures*.

PREFACE

Darkness.

Night comes with each orbit around the sun and, for most people on the planet, brings darkness with it. As beguiling as it can be, darkness is not empty. It is full of things, some seen and some not. It is the reason why we can live, for a human life without any darkness—artificial or otherwise—would quickly result in our being very ill and eventually perishing. We are creatures that need both light and dark to sustain ourselves. Beyond this rather literal description in relation to the quantity of light available, darkness has many other meanings too. It is intertwined with the night to such an extent that they have almost become shorthand for one another. Though just as night is so much more than darkness, darkness is considerably more than night. Darkness speaks, sometimes barely perceptibly, of other realms. It is where we originate from, inside the womb, and from it our lives truly begin. It is also found at the bottom of our oceans, in our deepest caves, and it stretches distances far beyond our known universe. It provides sanctuary and safety for many species that we share the planet with. It is an individually experienced phenomenon that is also universal. It transcends time and space to be a domain of awe, desire, and unknown possibility. Darkness can often appear magical. It can be the arena of wonder, creativity, freedom, and exploration. Boundlessly so.

Yet darkness has other connotations. It is also entwined with notions of evil, danger, ignorance, and oppression. We often fear the darkness. It is frequently perceived as the harbinger of all that might be bad in the world, where the very worst things could happen, and our senses sharpen with its potential threats. It is alloyed historically to primitive thought and cultures. It is baked into ongoing negative portrayals regarding issues of race. We refer to Dark Ages as periods of ignorance and error. Being in the dark—physically or metaphorically—is viewed as regressive and suggests a removal from what is conceived as good. Darkness can seem to remain terrible in its nature, and this is a double setback if we seek to reclaim it as a positive force. On the one hand, darkness is commonly perceived as a realm in which unspeakable acts of terror and violence might occur. On the other hand, the very idea of darkness also seems to reside as a bottomless pit in our imagination from where supernatural malevolence can rise at any time. For humans, it is our earliest and longest enemy for what it could conceal, as well as an entity that we could be afraid of in its own right.

Thinking about these contradictory relationships is why this book is now in front of you. In the name of progress, we have all but detached ourselves from the natural rhythms of the world, as we have sought to banish darkness from our lives. Day and night have become increasingly ambiguous as artificial light has blurred their boundaries. In the process, the convenience of artificial light has enabled us to overlook the true cost of how this impacts us and the countless other creatures with whom we share the planet. Many of us can no longer access the wonder of a starry sky, if indeed we have ever had the opportunity to experience one. Plus, as a species, we have not been satisfied with littering Earth and exhausting its resources, but are now putting more and more detritus into outer space. We have become so obsessed with conquering darkness in our lives that it has been beaten out of sight by light. In our brightly lit cities, as the night sky is aglow with light pollution, it is tempting to believe that there is little darkness left. But it is still there. Waiting. It is simply our access to it that is limited. While this barrier may seem permanent, it could be temporary. We have a choice and agency to do something about this situation. Dark skies used to connect us and provide a vital reminder of our position within the wider context of the world. It is hard not to be awestruck when we experience a dark sky. Fewer and fewer of us do so now. We have frayed our cord with the cosmos in favour of tethering ourselves to digital devices, luminous screens that not only divert our attention but also disrupt our sleep. It is a bitter irony that the very things that connect us to each other, in a digital sense, often further delaminate us from the world around us in many ways.

In an unprecedented era of climate emergency, we need to fundamentally rethink what we do, how we do it, and why. This book argues that the age of gleaming futures—allusive yet elusive shiny mirages of progress—is over. This is not a bad thing. Quite the opposite. It is time to think much more carefully about us, the planet, and all the species we share it with. We already know that the latter are in rapid decline, albeit with cascading effects that are not fully known. Suffice to say, if we carry on with a business-as-usual approach to everything, it is not going to end well for us. It is not too late, but we are certainly overdue for radical approaches to ensure that collective life, human and nonhuman, can thrive rather than merely survive. It is not an understatement to suggest that even this second option appears increasingly precarious and questionable.

Embracing darkness is about so much more than tackling light pollution. In fact, it runs through everything, and I do mean *everything*. Our ideas and ingenuity, our relationships and responsibilities to others, our innovations and their implementation. Together, these represent our capability to flourish or perish. Extinction is not an enticing option. We must do things differently. But where to begin? In this book, I propose that we completely rethink our relationship with the dark. By doing so, we can revitalise our imagination and our ability to create and deliver alternatives for how we live together, humans and nonhumans alike. This is essential and urgent amidst the increasing instability of our collective futures. Now, more than ever, we need to change. Dark futures, therefore, offer ways of thinking and doing towards positive change for everyone and everything. Come find me in the shadows; we have a lot to discuss.

The traces of this book are drawn from a lifelong fascination with the dark. From childhood play at dusk to over thirty years of nightwalking as an adult. Within the edgelands of Greater Manchester during my teenage years, through travels to many wonderful and occasionally overwhelming cities around the world, and back to the micro-geographies of movement that the pandemic made necessary, the nocturnal city has been a faithful, if ever-changing, companion. There is so much to enjoy here in the world after dark; I hope this book inspires you to do so in whatever way is practical.

Before we encounter more ideas, I would like to briefly divert the reader's attention to the format of this book and its contents. The book has a dual function. It seeks to critically examine specific arenas through which our relationship with darkness can be understood and to reflect on its themes, providing a personal narrative alongside the various discussions. It is arranged as a series of essays that consider different relationships with darkness across ideologies, ecologies, and technologies. Parallel to these essays are reflective writings that share my experiences with the dark and offer a different kind of narrative arc to the book. Key to these is the recognition that while aspects of darkness may be universal, the specific relationship each of us has with it is partial, relational, and situated. By sharing these personal encounters, it is my intention to illustrate various ways through which my relationship with darkness has been shaped and continues to evolve. Despite expressing my sheer wonderment of darkness in some of these passages, I also emphasise its beauty within the ordinary 'everynight' and make it relatable. This is, of course, my story of the dark, and I acknowledge the good fortune of being able to share it with you.

This is because I believe that dark futures concern all of us. So it is my intention to provide something open and provisional rather than closed and definite. These descriptive accounts start from where I live and then take in various places in the wider city of Manchester and its conjoined twin, Salford. There are two main reasons for this. Firstly, as my home city, the walks relayed from Manchester enable me to bring attention to the familiar and, crucially, the urban, which I believe forms a critical yet somewhat overlooked domain when we think about darkness. Secondly, despite its many different nocturnal ambiances, as a city it is simply not currently possible to experience dark skies in Manchester due to the large amount of light pollution; these passages seek to resonate with most readers of this book, since they too are unlikely to regularly experience pristine darkness. By connecting the wider themes of the book with personal experiences, I hope to encourage you to reflect on your own encounters and start new conversations concerning our relationship with darkness and its relevance for us, the planet, and the many species we share it with.

INTO DARKNESS

INTRODUCTION

We dream in darkness.

We arrive in the world, having journeyed from the bodily darkness of our mothers. We are brought into the light. The shock of this new, cold, and bright environment is profound. We may well cry. Over time, we learn the rhythms and patterns of life. We go about our days and nights, learning and accepting the circumstances of the world around us which shape who we are, what we do, and how and why. Under less scrutiny nowadays is *when*. The conveniences of our contemporary lifestyles belie some of the decisions that have been made in their development and our willingness to make use of them. As a species, our curiosity and ingenuity have led to major breakthroughs in the knowledge and understanding we have. Whether through branches of scientific discovery or the meaningful contributions made across arts and culture, we have literally changed the world and, in turn, reshaped our sense of selves. The relentless pursuit of progress has proved highly beneficial in many cases. It has produced ways to treat diseases and illness, transformed how we are connected to one other, and fundamentally shifted what it means to be human. We should rightly be proud of these achievements and the benefits they have given us. But ... it is this same impulse, however, that has also led to catastrophic events, environmental degradation, inequalities, poor mental and physical health, and climate change. A seemingly unquenchable thirst for the new and the next has resulted in resource extraction without restraint, multiple forms of pollution, endangering human lives and those of other species towards existential risk. If this doesn't sound good, it might be worse than we think.[1]

We cannot carry on this way.

Things must change.

How can we respond to the challenges set before us?

Let us first consider time and space. Both appear so infinite. Now let us think about darkness and place. Suddenly, our view of the world becomes much more situated and relational when we start to think about these two things together. Using the word *dark* as part of a term, however, can be seen as problematic for many reasons. Darkness is heavy in its association with other things. It tends to have a negative pull, bringing other words down with it (such is the apparent weight of the historical and cultural baggage attached to it). Dark ages. Dark days. Dark forces. Dark humour. Dark tourism. Dark web. For as long as we have been around, we have struggled with darkness. From our primeval origins to the present day, the dark is widely comprehended as unsettling. To reclaim the dark as a source of positive, progressive conceptual thinking is no small task. It compels us to look deep into ourselves, our histories, our cultures, and our values. We may not like everything that we find in there. It may be uncomfortable for us to question the structures and fabric of our beliefs and our societies. Yet I believe it is a vital key to unlocking a rebalanced relationship with each other, our countless nonhuman neighbours, and the planet. This book proposes a new philosophy for how we might think of the future, respond to the complexity of the world and its challenges, and how to safeguard the collective life that inhabits it.

What happens when, both metaphorically and literally, the lights go down? Rather than more is more where light is concerned, are we capable of having a different relationship with darkness? Since the Enlightenment, Western culture, especially, has been intrinsically bound with ideas concerning illumination and a reductive worldview that does not account for the diversity of experience and perspectives evident around the world.[2] In the context of many cities in the West, and increasingly in urban centres elsewhere, darkness is unwanted, connected as it is to negative cultural and historical associations alongside contemporary attitudes towards fear and crime. Although generally Western in their origin, values of light and its implications of clarity, cleanliness, and coherency have since been transferred across the global experience of culture more widely. This has resulted in a decline of how we perceive and understand darkness, to its detriment.

Likewise, when we consider what futures are possible, we tend to be directed towards visions of either a shiny, frictionless world which is light and bright or, at the other end of the spectrum, a fearsome, shadowy dystopia where darkness is essential in the evocation of decay and danger.[3] This book reclaims darkness as a lens for thinking about alternative futures which are neither technologically evangelical nor environmentally catastrophic. Instead, the concept of dark futures sketches out a third way through which we reconsider ourselves, our world, and the many species we share it with very differently. It proposes a new approach that embraces gloom as an emancipatory place for positive thought and creative expression as a platform for developing the appropriate commitment and actions for beneficial change.

THE PROBLEM WITH DARKNESS

This book encourages us to rethink darkness's role in our lives for the benefit of ourselves, our planet, and the collective life we share it with. Such a task requires many of us to reimagine and reconfigure our relationship with the dark in multiple ways. Yet if we are to reclaim darkness as a positive element in our lives to be valued for the common good, then we must also look at the issues it raises rather than ignore them. Darkness. It is always there, somewhere. Lurking, often unbidden yet deep with threat. As humans, we are historically and culturally conditioned by the places where we live, the people who raise us, and those we share experiences with. Our nature and nurture. For many people, darkness has lots of negative associations. It is widely perceived as the opposite of light and therefore antithetical with all that is supposedly good in the world. This binary relationship has endured. For our ancestors, when the sun went down, it was possible to be beset with all manner of potential hazards, as landscapes were less easily defined, predators better concealed, and human eyes simply not as effective in the nocturnal hours.[4] The night, in short, was dangerous. Moonlight would have appeared much brighter in contrast to how many of us might experience it today, due to the impact of artificial illumination at night, yet as a guiding light to the darkened world, the moon was still dependent on clear skies and favourable weather conditions. The ability to make fire had all kinds of benefits, not least the creation of artificial light. Suddenly, all kinds of new possibilities presented themselves. Parallel to the history of human progress is the development of artificial lighting technologies. As a species, our increased ability to colonise the night has enabled us to dominate large swathes of landscape for our benefit. Through this process and its accompanying succession of technological developments, artificial light has become synonymous with progress. The flipside of this, of course, is that darkness has continued to be deemed undesirable and problematic. There is much to celebrate in terms of humankind's knowledge and skill, not least our resourcefulness. But with its greater and greater impact upon the environment and all living beings, the unchecked use of artificial light needs to be challenged, and more fundamentally, our relationship with the very nature of light itself re-examined.

This narrative conceals other relationships with the dark throughout history. It is possible that darkness is simply too essential and, perhaps, overwhelming to us to be able to acknowledge it. Darkness represents the opposite of light-oriented words we depend on to convey understanding. Amidst the dark is the unseen, unformed, and unknown. A persistent association with darkness is fear.[5] We assume that fear of darkness is a part of our evolutionary development, perhaps even embedded in our DNA as a species. This fear is widely represented in folklore, mythology, and religion. If we think about the natural phenomenon of darkness, it is useful to recognise that there are different types of it. These are often related to different levels of visibility for different people. Rather, it is more helpful to talk about various degrees of darkness that reflect a spectrum of categories. Darkness is not the same in different places, just as night is not uniform. A scale does exist to measure the darkness of the night sky, which is one way to understand variation. Created by John Bortle in 2001, the Bortle Dark-Sky Scale ranks the night sky from 1 to 9, where 1 is assigned to those places that are truly dark, and 9 is the rating applied to highly light-polluted inner-city skies.[6] However, such categories don't make a great deal of sense in terms of how most of us relate to darkness, since this is shaped by our perceptions and experiences rather than measurement. Indeed, relationships with the dark are often specific and relative. Being in darkness might be frequently accompanied by other environmental characteristics such as lower volumes and different types of sound.

Total darkness might be conceived as the visual equivalent of silence. There are numerous accounts of silent retreat in dark places across diverse cultures. Retreats in complete darkness have been part of religious practices in the Tibetan Buddhist tradition since at least the fifteenth century. In the religious context, the dark environment is considered a better location for meditative practices because it enables mental visualisations without outward visual distraction. However, experiencing darkness in a solitary way is very much a matter of context. For as much as they might promote tranquillity and inner peace, the same conditions can also be applied as a form of punishing deprivation. When we are in darkness, we withdraw from our reference points in the world. Immersed in this apparent vacuum of outer experience, our inner experience becomes heightened. It is perhaps not surprising then that darkness fosters memory, since without additional stimuli, our ability to generate new memories is significantly reduced. Immersion in darkness beckons this reflection, an increasingly rare opportunity in contemporary life.[7]

Darkness is a pre-eminent characteristic of human experience that has become much maligned and is rapidly disappearing. It is intimately connected to the evolution of life, including humans. Our relationships with the dark are historically rich, yet only recently has archaeological and historical literature begun to acknowledge this.[8] Over the centuries, accompanying waves of technological developments were shifts in attitudes and values towards darkness. Moving from its primal origins, the fear and perception of the dark took on different interpretations. For example, in Ancient Greek mythology, Erebus is both the personification of darkness and the god of a dark region of the Underworld. Through intercourse with Nyx, the goddess of the night, they produce both Aether and Hemera, personifications of the bright upper sky and the day, respectively. Meanwhile, in the ancient Chinese philosophy and religion of Daoism, the emphasis on complementary relationships between light and dark led to a balanced appreciated of their coexistence. Clearly our ancestors had different relationships with darkness.

In the Middle Ages, darkness bore witness to considerable nocturnal activity. An alternate realm, night offered a refuge from ordinary existence and the realities of daily life. Essentially a time of freedom and renewal, the night and the accompanying darkness enabled men and women to articulate and act upon their innermost impulses and desires.[9] Although the night was far from a safe place, many people were reinvigorated with the onset of nightfall. It is little wonder that a series of repressive measures were implemented by church and state as an attempt to limit if not prevent activities at night. It was only toward the eighteenth century that initial steps were made in cities and towns to make public spaces accessible after dark. Make no mistake, darkness in medieval times was very potent. Aside from the impacts of religious beliefs and fears of the supernatural, the darkened landscape had considerable hazards including, but not limited to, fallen trees, steep hillsides, and open trenches. Settlements such as towns and cities, meanwhile, might contain ditches, piles of rubbish, and excrement-laden streets. While stories, songs, and proverbs were shared with young children to put them on guard about the perils of the night, as they got older, they underwent increasing exposure to life after dark through evening chores and errands. By doing so, older children became accustomed to darkness, improving their nocturnal navigation, and forming a healthy respect for the dark and the night. People during this period generally had a much more intimate relationship with their surroundings and the rhythms and details of nature.

Even with access to artificial light via lanterns or torches (usually makeshift in the case of poor people), many relied upon the night's natural conditions. The world after sunset was subject to many variations, from black gloom to the luminous glow of a full moon. Some of these subtleties would simply be too nuanced for our modern eyes to appreciate. Ascending at dusk and falling at dawn, a full moon could provide travellers at night with the capability to discern the landscape around them and its features in detail. If the moon was absent, then the natural light of the stars, albeit much fainter, could be relied upon, appearing both brighter and more plentiful than we can view them today. Moon and starlight were, of course, subject to the vagaries of cloud conditions, which could quickly change the amount of natural light and ability to make sense of the nocturnal world. On those nights when visibility was poor but wayfaring still necessary, people relied on their other senses to hear, smell, and touch their way through darkness. From our contemporary position, where sight dominates how we make sense of the world around us, it may seem strange to us yet in the early modern era that the use of our multisensory apparatus was vital to everyday existence, especially after sunset. The constraints of the daytime, meanwhile, were loosened. Despite the dangers of the night, in preindustrial times, it offered the primary arena of autonomy to many people. Balance was keenly appreciated, with darkness not necessarily problematic nor light a given blessing. The social landscape was revolutionised routinely by night. As the lower classes were released from their work and the scrutiny of superiors, darkness reversed some of the power dynamics. Instead, their associations were by choice, spending time with family and friends. This might seem modest to us now, but the hours of darkness presented a fundamental time across which the places and spaces of highly valued personal freedoms could be exercised without obligations to the powers that be. Coexisting with light and dark was essential to everyday and everynight life. The opportunity that emerged, as dusk transitioned from day to night, offered possibility and flexibility that was seized upon in all manner of ways by people exploring their inner and outer selves.

By contrast, the Enlightenment movement in Europe during the seventeenth and eighteenth centuries ushered in a powerful, moralising tone that redefined this relationship without any ambiguity. Light was pure: goodness itself, the very essence of wisdom, clarity, cleanliness, virtue, and truth. Darkness, by contrast, was everything that was bad with the world: evil, ignorance, falsehood; dirty, dangerous, and demonic. This shift was not only religious but also cultural, as the night became increasingly populated, and alongside this was the desire to reduce darkness. On a domestic scale, darkness was a problem because it made cleaning difficult, allowing bacteria and dirt to build up. Darkness, in this sense, becomes synonymous with ill health. Beyond the scale of interiors, urban darkness intensified concerns about moral decay, debauchery, and crime, fuelled by sensational media reporting. The increasing illumination of public spaces at night enabled the exposure and inspection of civil conduct.

The acceleration of technological progress through industrialisation not only transformed our ability to work but also had profound impacts on our environment. Suddenly, the appetite for the planet's material resources grew exponentially and, coupled with the exploitation of waterways and the creation of railway networks and trading links, expanded and sped up. Landscapes were irrevocably changed, our relationship with time increasingly measured artificially alongside productive capacity. Crucially, the night and its natural darkness was no longer an obstacle to the means of production. Quite the opposite. Now darkness could be obliterated for the purpose of creating capital.[10] The distinction between day and night diminished. Artificial light helped shatter darkness's role in our lives, reducing it to a mere inconvenience. People could be summoned to work around the clock in shifts, enabling non-stop labour. In the newly mechanised landscape of the industrial city, the night was the final frontier to be conquered, presenting itself as an extension of the daytime for work, social behaviour, and, increasingly, leisure.

Night was no longer a time of respite and recuperation from the day. Our natural rhythms with the wider world became somewhat frayed; sunset did not mean bedtime, nor was dawn necessarily a signal to rise for the day ahead. Indeed, night became a place of increased activity, work, and play. Yet these pursuits were reflective of social standing and represented the established hierarchies of power and privilege in terms of who did what and when they did it. As the boundaries between night and day became more and more blurred, the widespread availability of incandescent bulbs and access to electricity changed everything. Across the twentieth century, the electrification of artificial lighting technologies both within and beyond the home banished darkness to all corners at the flick of a switch. Increased levels of light were to be found outside via streetlamps, signage, illuminated billboards, and the growing number of vehicles moving through the night. Time, like space, could be occupied by people, and this was increasingly evident at night and no longer confined to the day.[11] Inside houses, additional lighting arrived courtesy of television sets and other consumer products with illuminated displays. As the century progressed and gave way to the next millennium, these beaming home invaders were subsequently aided and abetted by the screens of computer consoles, then laptops, smartphones, and other handheld devices. And here we are. Now into the third decade of the twenty-first century and our thirst for light still seems unquenchable.

Recent technological developments have been quick to set out their benefits, often with an emphasis on economic savings, without worrying too much about the other costs that artificial light can have. We have astonishing levels of light in numerous aspects of our lives, yet the growth and change of source of this artificial luminosity has largely gone unnoticed by most of us, while for some it has serious detrimental effects.[12] This increase in artificial light has been quiet but pervasive. We are now at a stage where we are fully accustomed to this lightness and brightness. And it presents a serious conundrum. Our view of progress as a species has led us to this point, where to reduce our use of light is often portrayed as regressive. Further complicating matters is that, even if we wanted to go back to a situation with a better balance of light and dark, do we even know what that is, and could we even agree on it?

The clue to starting this process lies above us between sunset and sunrise. Enchantment with the night sky is woven into the story of what it means to be human. The history of our connection with dark skies is rich and diverse. This relationship spans across time and space. It has shaped and been shaped by culture, religion, science, and society. In addition to the scientific knowledge that astronomy provides, artists, poets, and philosophers have been inspired by the stars, moon, planets, and universe. Throughout history, dark skies have provided an important domain in which we look for meaning in our lives. Although there is no clearly defined origin as to how or why humans began to relate to dark skies, a growing body of evidence suggests that this started around 70,000 years ago, roughly the same time as modern humans had evolved.[13] Before the advent of modern science, the relationship between an individual and the sky at night was usually immediate and awe-inspiring. Cloud conditions permitting, the stars were clearly visible, and common beliefs as to their purpose would be the basis for cosmic understandings between what was happening up there and down here on Earth. Australian Aboriginal meanings and uses of dark skies, for example, go back at least 65,000 years. Unlike the tendency in Western cultures, which uses written accounts to build and share knowledge in an objective manner, these oral traditions enable practices and understandings to be communicated in a way that retains their dynamic and protean qualities.

For millennia, humans were connected to dark skies. The star-filled night was celebrated and worshipped, an essential element to the invention of heaven and organised religion. Darkness played a vital role for the sacred rituals and other cultural practices of our ancestors. Being out at night and in darkness was powerful in shaping human actions and beliefs across different societies in the past. Experience in darkness often led us to establish cosmological connections, whether with the night sky, spirit beings, or our ancestors. In addition to observations of lunar and stellar phenomena, darkness presented a realm for socialising and other practical activities including nocturnal agriculture, fishing, sailing, raiding, and writing. Various societies referred to the night sky to schedule events or set ritual calendars. The night, therefore, with all its different kinds of darkness, as well as the light found in darkness, such as that of the moon and stars, produced significant behavioural, emotional, perceptual, performative, and ideological effects.[14]

Dark skies still provide immeasurable awe, reminding us of our place within the universe and our origins, as well as our possible futures.[15] This connection to deep time and the wonder of the cosmos is disappearing. Access to dark skies is increasingly limited, if not completely prohibited, in some places due to various forms of light pollution. An unintended by-product of our technological prowess has cut the bond between our species and the hallowed night. Irrespective of theological positions, it is difficult not to be overwhelmed by the beauty and wonder of a dark sky and its celestial objects. Aside from the spectacle itself, encountering darkness in this way can also stir up something more fundamental about our being on the planet.[16] Yet for a growing number of people, there has been an extinction of this experience.[17] This loss is not absolute but challenging to overcome. It becomes trickier, since more and more of us have never had the opportunity to experience dark skies firsthand and so are simply unaware of their majesty.[18]

To miss out on natural wonders is one thing, to damage the planet's ecosystems including our own health is another. Light and dark are essential to our circadian rhythms. As diurnal creatures, we are usually active in the daytime. As with most other diurnal animals, human activity-rest patterns are endogenously controlled by biological clocks. For thousands of years, most people went to sleep after the sun went down and became wakeful as it rose in the sky. With the advent of artificial illumination, this relationship was profoundly altered. We could control light and vanquish darkness.

We were able to extend our activities beyond the daytime and into the night. This also provided new opportunities for the nocturnal hours beyond rest. The distinctiveness between day and night, light and dark lessened. During the Industrial Revolution, the non-stop pursuit of capital also heralded the end of sleep. Suddenly shift workers could operate seamlessly around the clock. Aside from the air and noise pollution that such processes produced, artificial light became synonymous with our detachment from the natural rhythms of our ancestors.

Through the guise of progress, as moths flicker to a flame, we were drawn to this new version of the world and its splendour. For many, this was enforced labour, though it also opened up leisure and social possibilities. Amidst this wonder, our relationship with the night changed. We understood the value of light in casting out darkness in the pursuit of pleasure. Where it was deployed, darkness added drama and tension. In rare instances, darkness provided a convivial form of pleasure-seeking, such as in the Vauxhall Pleasure Gardens in London between 1729 and 1859. However, after dark it also provided an ideal site of transgression, excess, and illicit encounters. In my home city of Manchester, a similar experience was possible when, in the 1700s, a local man named Robert Tinker decided to clear and convert an area of land considered wild and neglected into Elysian Gardens. Established in the 1790s and continuing until the 1850s, the pleasure gardens were a significant place for people to enjoy during both day and night, with the gardens adorned by three thousand coloured lights. This amount of illumination might sound enormous when viewed from our current perspective, but these lights were very low in power, resulting in a sublime nocturnal experience of landscape.[19]

All too often, however, the veil of darkness enabled the furtive and forbidden to occur. It is perhaps no surprise that gas lamps were initially damaged in Paris and London, as it was felt by the perpetrators that they shed too much light on their nocturnal dealings. This colonisation of the night led to an increased appetite for greater spectacle. More was more! The urban night gladly gave it. Illuminated signs and shopfronts, streetlamps and traffic signs, an increasing array of neon, sodium, incandescent and fluorescent lighting transformed the urban landscape.[20] In some cities, searchlights swept across the sky or produced powerful fixed beams of light, illuminating upwards into the sky, to announce the spectacle of the urban night.

The illuminated city at night was mesmerising; the nocturnal hours became electrified, both physically and symbolically, as the modern metropolis and its glowing aura held the darkness back. The lure of the electric night was palpable; it energised the city and its people. It provided inspiration for artists, architects, filmmakers, photographers, poets, writers, and many others who sought to capture the atmosphere and explore the potential of this new phenomenon.[21] Further dynamism was brought via the headlights of vehicles—the urban night was a place in flux, ebbing and flowing, glistening and glowing. As the city reinvented itself from the day, the opportunity for people to slough off their daytime identity and enter the realm of the night was seductive. For many, such a release was vicariously enjoyed through their window as they went about their evening routines and rituals. But the possibility was always there, shimmering in the bejewelled fabric of the nighttime city.

The competition for attention in the urban night led to dazzling and ostentatious displays, colourful and bright, kaleidoscopic compositions to behold. Such brilliant and gleaming nightscapes were largely the preserve of entertainment districts, retail zones, and prosperous downtown areas. Light here also symbolised wealth. By contrast, the poorer neighbourhoods of the cities were often allied with darkness, itself now a signifier and determinant of urban differentiation. Older lighting technologies, where they had been installed, retreated into the distant streets and unfamiliar places, shadowy and belittled in comparison to the new. This difference only served to reinforce the binary relationship between light and dark. In the brightly lit districts, life's delights awaited you. In the gloom of the modern city, only bad things were potentially lurking. Thus, more and more light whenever and wherever possible. It became deeply connected to notions of safety, physically and psychologically. As it rendered all things visible, the dangers of the city were perceived as banished to its unlit margins and deprived quarters. This surveillance culture tapped firmly into historical beliefs concerning the unseen and unknown.

Consequently, the levels of artificial light in developed cities at night rose at a staggering rate. Enchanted by this new world after sunset, we barely noticed this greater and greater increase and our steady removal from the natural world and its rhythms. In fact, we became so used to it that the only real solution appeared to be ever more ingenious ways of illuminating the urban landscape to become even brighter and brighter. As the technologies became more efficient and easily distributed, their economic impact was reduced. But this was not the true cost of light.[22] One of the big challenges facing us is that we simply do not know the full extent of the problems light pollution is causing. Of course, this assumes we recognise it as an issue in the first instance.

If we were to turn on a tap in our home and coloured liquid flowed out, we would understandably be alarmed. Likewise, if when we walked down the street, we could smell gas leaking out of pipes and drifting through buildings, we would be extremely concerned about how hazardous our immediate surroundings might be. However, the pervasive presence of light pollution in many places has continued to grow, barely detected by most of us. Meanwhile, its impacts have been increasing but without us really understanding the consequences of the brightness we have bought and brought into our homes. This clearly has to do with both knowledge and choice. Lots of people around the world might not realise that light pollution is a problem. In this regard, perhaps many of us are rather like the metaphorical frog getting cooked in a pan of tepid water as the temperature slowly rises—the sinister threat arising gradually without us really noticing until it is too late.

We might be so accustomed to having an abundance of artificial light in our lives that we do not even think about it. In those situations where some people do recognise it as an issue, they might have limited options for what they can do about it. This is especially the case in contexts where rudimentary infrastructures providing energy, including that used for lighting, may be informal and/or precarious and thus there are no alternatives. In those circumstances where energy infrastructures and lighting products and services are well established, the lack of awareness is a barrier which, once overcome, can put people in a confusing situation. This is because, as consumers, our choices have been driven by economic value rather than technical requirements, so if we are told we can buy a bright LED bulb that is equivalent to a high-wattage incandescent bulb for reasonable money, then we will often buy it without questioning whether it is what we need. Now multiply similar thinking across every household, street, neighbourhood, district, city, region, etc., and it is easy to see why we have ended up where we are in terms of the scale of the problem.

Artificial light at night can contribute to different types of light pollution. Many of us are perhaps familiar with the orange-yellow aura that emanates from cities at night, usually referred to as *sky glow*. It has come to characterise nocturnal urban landscapes and their environs. From outside the city, whether from a hillside or an airplane, it is possible to see how this glow and the punctuation marks of some of its sources stretch out across the land.[22] What is less evident through such views is the impact this light is having on ecosystems. Darkness is integral to biodiversity, and its disappearance is having far-reaching ecological consequences for other species. Nocturnal rhythms and behaviours of flora and fauna are disrupted as artificial light alters the sensory capacities of creatures to breed, feed, and migrate.[23] There have been high-profile cases of many migrating birds who, disorientated by electric lights, become victims of 'fatal light attraction' and crash into buildings. In addition, the rhythms of insects, including moths and fireflies, are also disturbed, as well as the migrating behaviours of sea turtles, bats, beetles, and salamanders. Coastal and maritime lighting, meanwhile, can suppress the colonisation of certain species while promoting harmful others to flourish and foul harbours, precipitating ecological disaster. So far, so bad. But these are not the dark futures this book hopes to orientate toward—end-times scenarios of existential annihilation. Bringing about the significant changes required to counter these kinds of impacts on collective life is going to mean that we must rethink our relationship with the darkness. Given that its presence is largely through a coexistence of light, it is worth discussing why the contemporary issues that can be caused by artificial illumination at night are so problematic.

With our innovation and advancements, humankind has increasingly delaminated itself from the rest of the planet.[24] Despite this apparent remove, we are not impervious to the impacts of light. Unlike darkness, light pollution is not merely bound up in cultural perceptions and social behaviours. There is a growing body of evidence regarding the problems that light pollution is causing for human health.[25] Exposure to LED lighting, which is an increasingly common feature in both internal and external environments, has been linked to chronic sleep and circadian disruptions. This is not because of LEDs per se, but more to do with the type of LED that has proliferated in our indoor and outdoor environments as an energy-efficient replacement for previous lamps. Specifically, the white-blue light that emanates from this type of LED causes us, and many other species, problems.

In 1998, the discovery of a new photoreceptor in the human eye, which subsequently turned out to be especially sensitive to blue light, changed our thinking and understanding of how light affects human beings. Today, we understand the many unique physiological effects of light, including influencing hormone secretion, heart rate, alertness, sleep propensity, body temperature and gene expression. This sensitivity to blue also proved to be more powerful in elevating body temperature and heart rate and in reducing sleepiness; studies have shown that human performance improves acutely after the onset of light exposure, both at night and during the day, with quicker auditory reaction times and fewer lapses of attention under blue light. This can obviously be beneficial in the right situations but disastrous in other contexts. Unnatural lighting conditions are proving to be increasingly invasive and intrinsic to multiple negative impacts on health, human and nonhuman.

Where can we go from here? Our capacity to deeply alter the world we live in has been shown before. As we know, this has been with mixed outcomes. Often this has resulted in some benefiting and others not. Beyond the significant inequalities that remain between people around the planet, there have and continue to be countless nonhuman bodies who have been adversely and disproportionately affected by what we have done.[26] Included in this vast and varied, more-than-human population are many sentient beings that are unable to make their voices heard against such change. It is not all doom and gloom. We have frequently made things better for the common good, albeit one that is primarily humancentric. It is now time to apply this ability to mitigate some of the worst impacts of climate change, enable future generations to flourish, and share our planet gracefully with those who cannot speak for it. Put simply, our collective future depends on new and urgent forms of collaboration, coordination, and cooperation. This is no small task and will require significant creativity and imagination. This is how I believe that dark futures will play an essential role in what happens next. They can help us go beyond our existing and long-established problems with darkness to evolve a coexistence that is resilient and sustainable, inclusive and equitable, human and nonhuman, local and global, then our futures can be healthy and vibrant. The changes needed for us to achieve this are overwhelming. They are what is known as 'wicked problems', in so far as they are so complex in some ways that they resist being solved. It is perhaps no surprise that we prefer to look the other way. Where to begin?

This book aims to try to answer these questions. To be clear— there is rich potential and an urgent need for us to reconsider our perception and relationship with the dark. The premise of this book, therefore, is to open up these possibilities and explore several key trajectories. My aim is to question existing, widely held perceptions of darkness, to unlock fresh ideologies that can empower alternative relationships with our ecologies and our technologies. Such a vast subject as darkness cannot be contained in one work, much as the galaxy cannot be held in a pair of hands. However, by setting out a new agenda and presenting compelling reasons why this is so vital, it is my intention to contribute to this conversation. Why now? I am an urban creature, with thirty years' experience working in cities at night, which has given me the opportunity to gain knowledge and insights into how urban landscapes can evolve and, of relevance to this book, *become*. There is currently little work being undertaken on regulating light pollution in most urban areas. This is a paradox, since this is where a lot of light pollution is created. Worse, by preventing their right to a dark sky, urban populations are further impoverished, given that they are already likely to be struggling to access wild places or even green spaces. As such, urban populations are now removed from the wonder of the wider world both during the day and at night. That most people affected by this are completely unaware of this theft of the night is worrying. Plus, we are not talking about a new phenomenon. In many urban areas, there are already second or third generations for whom access to the stars has been denied. So while the conservation and protection of darkness where it can be found is important, addressing what is happening in cities and towns is equally pressing, if not even more so. The solution is at our fingertips. It could be as simple as flicking a switch. And yet, we do not do this. Why? There is something deeper going on where darkness is concerned, which we need to discuss. It goes far beyond the relatively recent (in terms of Earth's history) issue of light pollution and across time and space to our earliest origins. Indeed, the very idea of darkness is troublesome.

For all our sophistication as a species, our genetic material is ancient. Long ago, it made sense to be afraid of the dark. As a primal fear, it was essential to survival to be wary of the world after sunset when our ancestors were vulnerable to attack and other dangers. Far better to stay within a cave and wait until dawn before venturing out. This fear is no longer integral to our survival, but it does have a name. Fear of the dark is known as *achluophobia*, its origins stemming from 'akhlús' the Greek word for 'darkness'. Towards the end of the nineteenth century, the term *nyctophobia* was defined, drawing on the Greek word for night. Although it more directly translates as 'fear of the night', it has become more commonly used as a term to describe the fear of darkness. Here we can already understand the conjoined nature and interchangeability of the two words *night* and *darkness*. This slippage is evident in many aspects of our language and reflects the entanglement between the two. For darkness is not simply an attribute of night, though it is often when we encounter it, and night is considerably more than darkness. This makes things complicated.

Darkness may be a characteristic of night, yet it offers so much more than this, permeating our understanding of the world across millennia, being present physically in certain places when it is not night, or providing conceptual and metaphorical bases for how we think about and explain things. Night, meanwhile, can also be a time-space where there is negligible darkness, attaching itself to all manners of things between sunset and sunrise. It is into the darkness we will go. This is not about banishing light. It is about embracing darkness. These two things have a tricky relationship as we shall see. So please join me as we step into the shadows of space and time, together, to understand how we can reimagine and reconfigure our lives for a better, more equitable and sustainable world. Yet if we desire to have a long-term form of collective life that enables everyone and everything to flourish, we need to start questioning our ideas about darkness.

CUSP

2 a.m. Sleep eludes me again. I lie in charcoal darkness. The room around me is fuzzy in its various greys. Beyond the glass window of my home, the rumble of heavy-goods vehicles on the orbital motorway arcs through the nocturnal world outside. This is Manchester, on a cold and cloudy night. As I step out onto the street, the sky is a yellow-grey blanket, hung across the city before it was washed clean, and the not-yet of tomorrow is another slow spin cycle of Earth away. Bright white light punches its way along the pavement and parked cars, due to the LED streetlamps installed a few years ago. The night is molten soft. It awaits fresh imprints. As I walk through the suburban shadowland, my boots skid-slide on the damp stone slabs underneath, dew-kissed by Nyx. The nocturnal limbs of trees lining the edge of the park disappear into the night above. Towards the horizon, constellations of red lights float above the landscape like vermilion fireflies held in the urban aspic. The aura of vertical progress as concrete, steel, and glass seeks to push the sky away. Nearby, a taxi driver slumbers on his reclined seat and a mud-smeared van clangs into view.

My footsteps move onwards to the glimmering city centre, the cool air embalming my face with the night. The urban canvas stretches ahead, taut with crisp autumn air and sharp geometries of light and shadow. Under the dark umbrella of a willow tree, two figures chat in the gloom, passing the amber dot of a joint between them as we briefly overlap in each other's noctuaries. Now the metropolis asserts itself against the night as multiple towers buttress hard against the cloud cover. Glowing rectangles hang high on the city's surfaces, flat lanterns providing portals into the micro-worlds of unseen others. Light is, in fact, everywhere, chasing down the night and pummelling darkness into the margins. The soot-covered death mask of the industrial city has long been jet-washed away. In its place, the shimmering blocks of offshored capital. And yet … around a corner, behind a fence, squirrelled within the façades of buildings, darkness sits, biding its cosmic time. Waiting. Wanting to be released from its sharp-edged prison of light.

The open maw of night stretches in every direction, its guttural sounds mixing with the undertones of the city's nocturnal ebb and flow. The otherworldly qualities of places after dark spill out due to the apparent emptiness of many of them; the weird and eerie sense of absence is palpable. A street cleaner steadily whirrs into view, its rotating bristles suddenly clacking with the detritus of another urban night. These are the pre-dawn ablutions that wash away the excesses of the hours after dusk. The city is but its people. So when they have all gone away, only the traces of them flutter about or are laid to rest in the crevices of the night. Bottles and cans ensconced within the niches of buildings, takeaway trays and crisp packets flouncing their way along the pavements. The human protagonists may have left the scene, but there are other bodies here: furry and furtive, feathered and flapping, flying, and feasting on the spoils of the night. Just because you were not there, does not mean it was devoid of life. The lichen and moss surreptitiously bloom at a glacial pace. The moment of time itself is enshrined in the promise of night. A slowing down. Stop. I take a deep breath. The sharp tang of fox urine reanimates the world, everything flows again, and the shiver of the street as I walk along it bobs in tandem with my gait. The last transmissions from the site of the former BBC New Broadcasting House lost in the ether of many yesterdays. In its place, the lamentations of urban regeneration, fuelling high-rise dreams with low architectural ambitions. On the sorrow goes, grieving skyward in banal weeps.

24

Shifting from the main road, the downward slant of a side street takes the feet steadily into its rhythm. To the left, the brick viaduct assuredly strides behind buildings to span across the city night, framed views of the metropolis are briefly held firm in its arches before their porosity is revealed by movement. To the right, the new (b)landscape of investor confidence written in towering blocks huddles together in collective embarrassment at their meagre offering to the street. There is no sanctuary to be found here, just the hard line—either you are inside or you are outside—exposing those on the street to the elements. The façade of a building can be a generous thing, articulate in its conversation with the wider built environment. Not here, though; the surfaces are blank and mute. Brief glimpses of the ghosts of past cultures, absentee landlords for the next generation to blossom out of the brickwork and beyond the shadows of the 1980s and 1990s. Smuggled in a nearby archway, two bodies rest in a tent, both adjacent to the cloud-pinching apartments yet also a world away from accessing them. We practise regret as practice perfects. Under the nocturnal commons, the inequalities might seem less visible, prone in the urban margins, but they are keenly felt and more explicit. An empty disposable coffee cup rolls, animated by the downward draughts that tumble onto the life between buildings unbidden. The street begins to rise as I turn towards the city's nucleus. Sharp shadows compete with the fuzzy yellow-white glow of urban ambiance, its nocturnal pallor smeared and scrubbed onto the cityscape.

Pause. Standing on the corner of a main thoroughfare, the city after dark slowly reveals itself, a long exposure image, straddling the past and stretching tentatively to the future, right here in the present. Yet somehow the anticipated future never quite arrives, either somewhat blurred or saturated with too much meaning to be fully formed. This is the secret of night. Darkness is both a promise and a premise to sustain this process of becoming. It enables the dissident, the radical, the deviant, the visionary to unfurl from the identity of the daytime and be present and active. As for me, tonight I am a wayfarer of ideas and of streets, my walking steadily stitching together half-opened pockets of my mind with those of the city. Memory, encounter, and imagination are the bedfellows of this time-space patchwork. The lingering aromas of Chinatown snap me out of my reverie. The road glistens with inaccessible neon portals on its surface, reflections of the world above. It is a microcosm of what darkness offers—an alternative universe of thought and potential—while also being essential to the reality of our existence here in the world. In the dark, we can experience the liminal zones between body and landscape, natural and artificial, place and time, humans and nonhumans, built and unbuilt, identity and rebirth. Darkness stirs ideas deep within us, both welcome and not.

Threading through the back streets, then along the perimeter of Piccadilly Gardens, the city peels away down a gentle slope. Another human being curls up in a doorway under a sleeping bag, a few more coins placed in the battered paper cup beside them perhaps providing some temporary respite or brief pleasure from the street tomorrow. At Cross Street, the tramlines glide their way along the road on either side of me to suburban lives outside of the city's shimmering promise. The river's gravitational pull draws the body to meet it. Onwards and downwards towards that animated swathe of black, the River Irwell. Manchester and Salford are stitched together here by its viscous ribbon. At night, the water seems unfathomable, its surface winking back at the increasing congestion of high-rise buildings on either side. Under the shadows of the vertical city, the dark dreams of a new future that might be forged. As diversity and differentiation in cities appear to be slowly, sometimes brutally erased, it seems that the margins might offer what the centre cannot hold. Forget utopia and its illusory shiny goodness. It is always out of reach, an unattainable mirage. Let us leave the debate of its failure or recuperation to others. This is a different approach. Rather than obliterate it, we need to be able to adjust to darkness for our collective future. More than ever before, it is essential we progress with darkness rather than continue its oppression. To achieve this ambition, we must reconsider what we perceive darkness to be. It is time to step into the darkness; futures await us and here we are—on the cusp between times.

DARKLING

THROUGH THE PAST, DARKLY

Over the years, I have grown to know the gentle dusk in my hands. Like fine gauze, it first slips between my fingers and brushes against my face, my hair, and my clothes. Before the onset of darkness, the dusk gathers around my boots in slowly accumulating clouds of charcoal candy floss. As the boundaries between my body and its surroundings blur, the darkness shifts its weight, leaning in for a hug. Now it's your turn. Think of complete darkness. With your eyes closed and lights off, the unlit room initially seems cast into a deep dark. Moments later, however, the formless and endless material gives way to soft shapes and subtle hues. The darkness gathers its skirts as light reasserts itself, abseiling along the edges of blinds and curtains, sneaking under the door, glowing from devices. The darkness settles and is familiar. Now try again. Think of complete darkness. Perhaps you are floating in outer space, nestling into a deep cave, or meditating in an ocean trench. How does it feel? Darkness is protean. It can move quickly through its moods or slowly unfold its different textures. Darkness stirs us. We can be in awe of its beauty and shrink from its threat. It is within us and beyond us, full of endings and beginnings. Our impressions of darkness remain in flux, changing over time, with mood and context, with climate and chance. We make sense of our environment in a very different way when the molten veils of darkness fold and fuzz the world around us.

As an adult, my relationship with darkness has evolved. My teenage years were spent with friends, mooching around the edgelands of the outer Mancunian suburbs after dark. Avoiding the casual violence of pubs and clubs, a trio of us would wander through the fields and woods, along former spoil tips, around abandoned buildings, and the sodium-fused suburban landscapes. Darkness was always close by. Astley, Atherton, Boothstown, Little Hulton, Tyldesley, places with corresponding postcodes that designated their distance from the city centre, M28, M29, M46, like deep-sky objects from the Messier catalogue. As we walked or sat around, we were immersed in the multisensory world after dark. We listened to the nocturnal soundscape's rhythms as they ebbed and flowed with our movements. Bits of the ordinary were transformed at night, oil puddles on tarmac sharing their iridescent swirls—galaxies in miniature embedded in the road; the soft fur of willow catkins announcing the oncoming spring—tiny shy creatures of otherworldly fluff in the gloom.

As the three of us went our separate ways after college, the lure of the dark still captivated me. I worked two part-time jobs to help support my studies in architecture. On Saturdays, I was an itinerant cashier for a small network of betting shops, filling in for staff shortages. Whatever the weather and light conditions outside these venues, the inside was always a smoky, dingy space. Time slowed down in here, brooding until the inevitable climax of the race punctured the air to reflect the fortunes and frustrations of the punters. The betting shops were like pockets of night—albeit a very particular type of night—manifest in the daytime. Emotions could ride high, elated or consolatory, raucous celebration or vague mutterings, as tempers bristled along a fine line between joy and misery. The smell of booze from punters using the nearby pub, the murky atmosphere and dark interiors were a world away from the daylit life beyond the door. Quite unintentionally, my eight-hour day job was like a long stretch of twilight, never quite leaving the daytime or arriving at night. Tears ran as I blinked myself back into the early evening after a shift, the smell of my smoke-soaked clothes wafting out as I moved down the street.

The other job, meanwhile, pushed me further into the dark corners of the city region. For five years in the mid-late nineties, I worked as a freelance crime scene surveyor. Although computer-aided drawing was steadily becoming adopted in various professions, the courts requested that supporting evidence was in the form of technical drawings produced manually. Forget the glossy sheen of detective dramas and action movies. The assignments I worked on were sites of condensed trauma in the city. Most places were domestic interiors and non-descript settings—banal spaces which had become pressurised containers to foment abuse and violence. Due to my commitments in the studio for my architecture degrees, some of the visits to these places were made after sunset. Being immersed in what seemed like a very different city from the one I had grown up in, the darkness here vibrated with the aftershocks of crime and neglect. I didn't think about it much at the time, perhaps as part of an unconscious self-defence, but the residues of this shadowy city would linger on far beyond the period in which I undertook the work. Nowadays we would refer to this as a form of post-traumatic stress disorder, but back then it was simply not discussed.

In later years, the echoes of some of the sites I had witnessed in the dimly lit spaces of tower blocks, houses, and gardens would sneak out of a fissure in the city due to the *déjà vu* invoked by a place. Whenever this happened, the memories were always edged with a dark fuzziness, as if this were an elemental aspect of the previous experience. Over time, this shivering matter would fade away from my recollections as largely did the memories themselves. For several years, however, my relationship with the nocturnal city oscillated between the sense of it as an arena for exploration and one which held its innermost terrible secrets. In hindsight, I think that the darkness in these mental images was a deliberate way to obscure some of the more disturbing details and provide a buffer between the real and the imaginary. The dark borderlands of my mind were beneficial. They provided a coping mechanism and showed me that darkness afforded protection rather than being something that contained a threat. It might sound strange, but I rarely thought about the night and darkness much while completing my studies in architecture. Perhaps that was part of my way of blocking out some stuff. Only fifteen years later did I return to this as a subject to be investigated, and that was by accident.

Following an uninspiring period working in architecture practice, I returned to university to teach part-time for several years. During the same period, I was also the frontman in a band, and my life was a schism. By day, I was a mild-mannered tutor, learning how to support others as they made their way through their own creative journeys in the world of architecture. After dark, however, I transformed into a vortex of black ink, denim, and boots as I writhed on stages around the land, fully committed to the noise-drenched sermons we were delivering. Darkness, at this point, came in two forms. Either as the artificial dark of small concert venues, the four of us emerging from shadows and into the stage lights to become action paintings of sound and bodies as we urged the crowd into our maelstrom. Or it was the long stretch of darkness as it bruised its way through its various blues to dawn as I drove our hired minivan back to Salford following a gig. The former was exhilarating, palpable darkness that quickened the heart and sharpened all the senses. The latter was dull dark, desperately trying to stay awake in the early hours and get four exhausted bodies home to bed, following the punctuations of streetlights and the curves of motorways that sliced through the charcoal night. Like any black hole, the band imploded. Meanwhile, after five years of precarious employment across several institutions, I was successful in obtaining my first permanent job. These two events may or may not have been related.

Like many jobs, over time my working life became denser with more and more roles and responsibilities, and personal tribulations harder to manage. Something had to give. One night, utterly despondent with what felt like an impossible situation with no means of escape, I took to the streets. The nocturnal city appeared sympathetic to my inner turmoil. As I walked through the dark streets, a place and time opened up through which I was able to explore my thoughts and restore balance. Since then, nightwalking for me has become living proof that amidst the darkness there is always meaning. In early 2014, coincidentally around the same time I began nightwalking regularly, the city council of Manchester, where I live, announced its intention to roll out a replacement of 56,000 streetlamps with LED ones. While no two nights are ever quite the same, suddenly the darkness of the city that had become familiar was under threat. The implementation of bright white LEDs in favour over the orange glow of sodium lamps was radically altering the city's nocturnal atmosphere. The ambiances that had accompanied Manchester after sunset were being changed quietly but with instant effects.[27] Darkness itself was being reconfigured in dramatic ways. Above all, the increase in light at night meant that darkness was further diminished. It was being hounded out of the city, the ambiance that had characterised the night for decades transformed by the switch of a bulb. There was significant nostalgia attached to the nocturnal city of orange-grey hues, the only versions I had ever known. Yet something felt off. Directional lights cast their bright beams down, and the ambient light levels grew and grew. Reinvigorated with a new sense of purpose, I decided to use some of my nightwalks to document the disappearing city of darkness.

Over the last decade, this activity has led to several thousand hours of walking through cities at night and the production of an archive of photographs, maps, and auto-ethnographic notes. I compiled this archive to capture some of the different ambiances of light and dark in urban places, and to show how these are changing. I am not the first person to undertake such research. In 1869, journalist Blanchard Jerrold, together with French artist Gustave Doré, produced an illustrated record of London's shadows and sunlight. They spent many days and nights exploring the capital, its night refuges, cheap lodging houses, and other locations of human nocturnal activity.[28] What began for me as enjoyment of the quiet and reassuring embrace of the city after dark has since mushroomed into a body of work that involves film, photography, sound recording, writing, talks, and yes, many more nightwalks. Although some of the latter have been collective events (taking a group of people around the nocturnal city to have positive encounters with urban places after dark), far more have been just myself communing with the darkness.

My current relationship with darkness, however, has not been one of mere practicalities for conducting field work at night. There are specific sensibilities in the nocturnal city that open creative exchanges between identity and place.[29] I am particularly interested in the multisensory experiences and aesthetics of urban nightscapes, how they are used and by whom, as well as their shifting dynamics. This poetry of the city after dark, the many threads it draws into its warp and weft, is what keeps me returning. The nocturnal city melds the real and the imaginary.[30] It offers a place for the personal and reflective, as well as collective effervescence. Darkness in urban places can be enchanting but also disorienting. Less fixed and predetermined than in the daytime, the open and provisional qualities of the city at night are fluid, fragile, and fleeting. Having taken many nightwalks around Manchester and the wider metropolitan region, I am still surprised and enamoured with how places that I think I know intimately can feel so different after sunset. The city after dark encourages us to embrace unexpected ways of engaging with the urban night, its ambiances asking us to imagine and sense its spaces differently. They can be lucid and supernatural, often oscillating between the familiar and strange, due to the interplay of light and dark as parts of a multisensory engagement with the world at night. As someone who studied architecture and has spent many years thinking about the designs of cities, I find this realm fascinating. Cities at night seem to hint at a future that hasn't quite arrived but is tantalisingly just out of reach, hovering in view between the brilliance and the gloom.

As with the endless wonder that the velvet night sky evokes, my work with darkness continues to unfurl in unexpected ways. It has led to collaborations with some of the most creative, generous, and kind people you could ever hope to meet, whose knowledge and expertise have helped me understand more about the importance of darkness. One aspect of this has been the realisation of how quickly natural darkness has been disappearing due to our obsession with light, without understanding its impacts. This is something this book explores in relation to three key themes: ideologies, ecologies, and technologies. It considers the ideas we have had concerning darkness and how they have powerfully shaped our perception of darkness, before looking at alternative ways of relating to it. The significance of natural darkness for various ecologies is subsequently shown across different environments to emphasise the impacts that artificial light can have and to illustrate the global reach of the problems we now face. It then examines the technologies of lighting, especially in relation to urban places, as a means of explaining how we have arrived at the contemporary city in all its illuminated splendour, proposing new ways to become re-enchanted with the urban night. But why take my word for it? Forty-odd years ago, a dark-eyed boy was looking out his window, wondering what was out there in the darkness. As far as that is concerned, I haven't changed much.

THE DARK TWIN OF CHILDHOOD

I wasn't always this way. My relationship with darkness has obviously changed over time. Standing on the outskirts of Manchester, viewed from this hill to the north, the city is a giant luminous creature. The circulations of this shared body gleam and pulse through the night against the continuous hum and glow of its basal metabolism. A gigantic illuminated conjoined nervous system, always so much more than the sum of its parts. Upon closer inspection, it is not one single entity. Peering harder, it becomes apparent that it is many organisms dancing together, locked in a choreography of collective effervescence. Taking a long slow look is always worthwhile. The loud and the bright compete for our attention—so where now the secret, the quiet, and the contemplative? This is what my previous book *Dark Matters* set out to explore by illustrating that beyond the lurid noises and screaming lights of the city at night, another city was also present. This dark twin of the daytime city had composure, sanctuary, and substance in its pockets. This book seeks to present a wider approach, to radically reconsider how we frame the dark in our thinking so that we might find alternative futures that are inclusive, ethical, and sustainable.

What might dark citizenry look like? Recognising that the places where we live and work—and the other species that, intentionally or not, coproduce such environments—requires us to take care of them. This endeavour should not disappear or diminish when we close the blinds, draw the curtains, or flick switches and tap apps to bring artificial light into the post-sunset dark. Outside, the natural world does not stop. We might close ourselves off from the outdoor environment, but on it lives, above, around, underneath, and away from our homes. It also lives on countless surfaces, in the cracks, out of view, or undetectable by human eyes. Nocturnal life is a manifold wonder, from the microscopic to global networks of migration by many different species. Yet we have also aided and abetted the incursions humans have made upon the night, whether consciously or not. Our always-on, non-stop, networked lifestyles have meant we have quickly become accustomed to the conveniences of rapid demand and supply goods and services. All this requires labour. It may often be unseen and unheard, but this labour continues to move within and throughout the night. Its geographies, rhythms, and temporalities may be out of sight, but it is the embodiment of the decisions we make with the tap of a screen. Such labour is not without its consequences. It is often precarious, poorly paid, and problematic in both the direct and indirect impacts that such work has on those performing it. So surely there is an ethics at work after dark? The connotations of 'dark' are seldom positive when it appears as a prefix to human activity: dark tourism, dark thoughts, or indeed, other realms such as the dark web or emerging phenomena such as the dark kitchens which are steadily appearing in and around cities to service their citizens. Each of these terms implies something away from mainstream or conventional, even acceptable, ways of doing things. Instead, these terms suggest notions of surreptitious, unsavoury, and even illegal functions; it is their out-of-sight quality that brings forth these associations because they are immediately recognised as being in the shadows—*dark*—and therefore perhaps not to be trusted or viewed as entirely legitimate operations.

This ongoing perception of the dark as problematic or somehow not quite honest and open is tricky to untangle. We correlate darkness with many bad things that have happened, real and imaginary, but this is not the same as causation. Much of this has to do with how we encounter and experience the dark. From an early age we are told to be afraid of the dark. In my own childhood, the onset of darkness often signalled the time to stop playing and go home. Once there, bedtime stories were full of things that went bump in the night, unseen or obscured by darkness, which enabled them suddenly to appear and wreak their havoc. It was relatively easy to make fun of these ghouls and monsters once the storybooks were closed. This did not, however, prevent me conducting a thorough inspection under my bed with a torch once I was left alone in my bedroom to go to sleep. These investigations felt hazardous, since they were tinged with the very real possibility (in my child mind) that the beam of light in my hand might sweep over something unexpected. Sometimes the skewed shadow cast by an ordinary object, as my torchlight scanned around my bed, would cause me to recoil until I could assure myself of the familiarity of its origin. Yet pursue this task I did until such a point that a more rational version of myself outgrew these worries and others crept into the void left behind. The dark had assailed my conscious and my subconscious.

Over time, my relationship with the dark evolved. In the early stages of my adolescence, in the 1980s, it signified the transgressive potential of late(ish) nights watching films rented from the local video store: turning the electric lights off to recreate the atmosphere of a cinema, the palpable sense of anticipation as I inserted the black VHS cassette into the top-loading video player, and the silence broken by its clunk and click followed by the whirring of the machine; the fuzz and distortion of the image as its screen of white, grey, and black settled into a coherent image and then the familiar intro music of the movie studio began. Those encounters, whether experienced alone or with friends, became significant portals through which the journey from a domestic interior to other worlds took place, replete with their aliens, monsters, and other forms of weirdness. The nature of such escapism often meant that the films chosen were usually science fiction and fantasy. Within these narratives, darkness was a frequent accomplice—as much to conceal dodgy special effects as to convey the often brooding, even malevolent ambiance that supported storylines with eerie if not evil creatures. In my young mind, this simply reinforced the idea, already depicted in books and comics, that darkness was where extra-terrestrial life and supernatural beings resided. The darkness of the room where the film was being watched would appear as an extension of the film set, a barely detectable membrane existing between reality and not reality. This was particularly unnerving when watching the film *Poltergeist* (1982). Yet it was not always necessary for films to be watched in darkness to become enveloped in them. One sunny afternoon, I drew the curtains and sat and watched *Alien* (1979) alone and was utterly consumed by the literal darkness of much of what happened on the screen, which was even more fearsome for its stirrings in the shadows and gloom. This material darkness appeared to leak out of the television and infuse the room. Although these experiences were personal to me, similar encounters with the dark shape many childhoods. They draw on those ancient and primal origins of darkness as the harbinger of bad things. Darkness also provides a realm for the creative and imaginary to roam, unfettered by the paradoxes and limits that light can bring.

The uneasiness of sometimes being with darkness was part of its allure. Perhaps it still is. The thrill of the dark is something that taps into our innate humanness with all its awkwardness, anxieties, excitements, and fears. It is the arena of the odd, wherein the everyday can quickly dissolve into an altogether very different premise. Our encounters with darkness thus shape us, and in turn, we shape it. This means that despite being a universal phenomenon, our relationship with the dark is individual. Although our physiological apparatus is broadly the same, our cultural conditioning, sense of identity, and previous experiences all contribute to how we encounter darkness and perceive it. Importantly, this is not fixed. Darkness is situated, relational, and plural. So it follows that our experiences of it vary, across the life course, where we are, who we are with (or not), what we are doing, when we are doing it, how, and why. For many people, being out and about at night feels very different in an urban setting from a rural one. Likewise, being alone can make one perceive the same space distinctly differently from when with amiable company.

Living in a suburban environment during my childhood meant that access to night creatures seemed limited. Adjacent farmland and former mining landscapes gave rise to manufactured and untamed places, respectively. Within those places, the nocturnal activities of nonhumans made themselves known in the hedgerows and fields, trees and grasslands, with forays into the brick and mortar, concrete and asphalt of suburbia. In the late 1970s and early 1980s, it was certainly darker at night than it is now. There was simply not as much light pollution in the urban environment, nor were the 24/7 on-demand consumer lifestyles underway. Likewise, the influence of pervasive digital technologies had yet to emerge in domestic settings, and children were largely left to play out until sunset. I can remember many evenings making my way back home as darkness began to cast its shawl across the landscape and the gloaming emerged around my friends and me. In these moments, being immersed in the no-longer-day-but-not-quite-night was exciting. The increasing blur between our surroundings and our imagination could quickly give way to a powerful sensation of being out of sync with the world and deep within a liminal zone that was not homely or even earthbound.

Signalling this transformation, the sodium lamps' warm tones would wash the landscape with their orange-yellow hues. Suddenly, a third space between here and the dawn would emerge. One that seemed full of possibility, difference, and was activated by the otherworldly glow of artificial illumination. A new place that was not day but somehow not night either. The tendrils of this domain cast their shadowy fingers across the pavement and streets. Buildings that several hours previously had been homes and familiar now appeared uncanny and less certain of themselves. The tiniest details of bricks and mortar or rendered walls would become epic landscapes of form and shadow as light moved or was halted across their surfaces. Asphalt roads, meanwhile, were no longer the banal strips of suburbia that allowed cars and vans to shuttle back and forth but were galaxies of orange-grey astral belts connecting the past and the future. Eventually, the voices of parents came tumbling over fences and around corners requiring us home. 'Make sure you are back before dark,' they had said, the phrase fizzing with undertones of undisclosed peril.

This seemed a strict line in time. A definite threshold in the cosmos. Yet, what precisely constituted 'dark' was open to interpretation. Was it the gentle buzzing of the streetlights coming on? Could it be when the gloam of the land seemed to rise and become one with our lower halves? Or was it the tiniest pinpricks of the stars apparent in the sky? Ill-judged (let's be honest, we were children and thoroughly absorbed in the immediacy of whatever we were doing), there could be a reckoning for not following instructions. Arguing in relation to the nuances of three types of twilight was beyond our ken back then, so it was usually a matter of multiple feet scuffing back together. Gentle blame would then be directed to absent friends when back at home if any of us were slightly later than anticipated due to this somewhat fuzzy boundary. A ginnel often formed part of our way back home. At either end, the orange glow of a road. But in between these, the channel formed by high garden fences made it seem very dark. Daring each other to go ahead, the excitement was palpable. Hearts in mouths, we crept forward as one, a many-limbed beast inching its way along the gloomy path. Then, inevitably, one of us would be unable to bear the tension any longer and suddenly run headfirst into the dark, and a scramble would ensue because none of us wanted to be last to leave the clutches of the shadows. Whatever imaginary thing was going to grab us was never clear. It did not need to have a name. The ineffable aspect of it formed part of the dread. Suffice to say, the darkness itself held mysterious and eerie qualities as if able to ensnare us. This unspeakable aspect of the dark fuelled tall stories and gripping childhood adventures, always second-hand stories passed on from someone's distant cousin or older sibling's friend of a friend. Our wide eyes and hungry minds were less interested in the provenance than in the spirited tales.

This melding of trepidation and lack of light quickly condensed. 'Lights out' became shorthand for summoning whatever might be brought forth in the wake of darkness. Mundane domestic noises suddenly took on spooky if not sinister mutterings; familiar textures became alien, the background elements of everyday life now recast into a spiralling tableau of the strange. Perhaps many of us can relate to this and recall similar stories from childhood. To do so would, however, only tell part of the tale. For there were also positive engagements with darkness in my suburban childhood, waiting quietly to see if foxes, owls, and bats would emerge, listening for the sounds of the nocturnal world and then looking upwards in complete awe of the universe's apparent endlessness. A young mind, like so many others, fascinated by space travel and the wonders of the sky at night. Darkness, for all its trickiness, was also a friend offering comfort, magic, and dreams. This dark twin of childhood was and is vital, yet it can become easily lost as we grow up and, more often than not, increasingly detach ourselves from the world around us.

ROOT

Midnight. I am standing by the former Hope Hospital in Salford. A little less than five decades ago, this is where I arrived in the world. From the darkness of the womb to the brightness of the hospital room. Babies had been born on-site since 1882 until 2011, when the maternity unit was closed. A subsequent, freestanding midwifery unit operated for a few years until 2017, then another freestanding birth centre opened its doors in early 2018. I follow the bow of Eccles Old Road to Buile Hill Park and cross the threshold under the dark foliage of trees that line the perimeter, its iron fencing that had stretched along the park boundary long since removed for the manufacture of bullets during the Second World War. In 1590, Hill Hart Meadow, which later became part of this park, was a plague burial site. It has an extensive history, but my memories of this place are deeply rooted in the dark.

In 1975, the Natural History Museum that occupied most of the Buile Hill mansion became the Lancashire Mining Museum. It was here, frequently during school holidays, that my younger sister and I would experience the underworld of the industrial revolution. It was a heady experience. Down into the blackened and gloomy spaces and into a labyrinth of exhibits featuring soot, filthy figures, and bits of machinery we would go. My sister held my hand tighter as we left the daylight behind and preferred not to make eye contact with the somewhat ghoulish faces daubed in black lest they move to meet our gaze. The pit pony, frozen in time by taxidermy, blinkered and straining as it pulled a wagon of coal up into the daylit world was the very opposite. This dark space was somewhat haphazard and ambiguous to young minds. It vibrated with an eerie quality, a wormhole of time and space between the present and a seemingly distant past that was recent. It certainly stirred up primal feelings in two children.

Moving across the turf, the downward tilt of the park guides me towards the glow of the civic centre of Salford and then Manchester city centre behind. Langworthy Road doubles down on the inner suburban landscape, tight-lipped terrace houses huddle together, only occasionally giving way to more recent development. Four teenagers lean against the side of a closed shop, the glow of mobile phones and cigarettes offering fleeting windows into their world. Meanwhile, the blue-greens of television screens leak out from behind curtains and blinds. The landscape opens as the road carries me above and beyond the M602 motorway and its sporadic stretches of noise. Homes have stopped in favour of light industrial buildings and business parks. Tramlines curve in to accompany my steps and sheen their way along the street ahead. The road stops, but the tramlines carry on, as do I, toward the mirage of Salford Quays. One of the first and largest urban regeneration projects since the 1980s, this area has brought with it an unbridled optimism and hotchpotch of buildings. The black mirror of the Manchester Ship Canal wobbles the lights of adjacent architecture.

Towards the Erie Basin, along the narrow strait of the Mariner's Canal, and adjacent to Ontario Basin. Exotic-sounding places, whispering of the industrial past. Navigating the sporadic thrum of the dual carriageway, I move along to Ordsall Park. The dark turf here is short and awaits the oncoming kiss of dew. Guy Fawkes Street, as my shadow weaves in and out of the railings that accompany the perimeter of Ordsall Hall. I can just about glimpse the Ordsall Peacock, a bronze sculpture that, despite its size and weight, managed to take flight for more than three decades but is thankfully reinstated in the area. Back along Ordsall Lane towards the gleaming towers that increasingly congregate against the sky. Over a footbridge and I am transported to

Pomona Island. Or what is left of it. The ghosts of its past are barely traceable now.

During the industrial revolution, this landscape was home to botanical gardens and the Royal Pomona Palace. Opened in 1845 and originally called Strawberry Gardens, it was an idyllic escape just south of the congested city centre. The abundance of horticulture led to the site being renamed Pomona Gardens, *after the Roman goddess of fruit. On 22 June 1887, the fate of Pomona's grand palace and gardens was sealed when a catastrophic explosion at a nearby chemical works resulted in the building being badly damaged. The island was then used as dockland until the 1970s, when the docks closed. A couple of short-lived attempts to bring human activity back to the island ended in 1981. Pomona was left to its own devices, a true island of abandonment, where biodiversity flourished without much human interaction. Beloved of wayfarers of various demeanours, Pomona Island became almost mythical. Visits to it over the years somehow always managed to stir the blood, especially at night when its otherworldly qualities and isolation from the city formed a sublime experience. The former things that coproduced this ambiance—the strewn and overgrown flora, the discarded detritus of people, the shadowlands of a place not well lit—created a zone that was much more than a wasteland.*

Pomona Island in some ways felt like the last refuge from the city— out of sight and out of mind as far as most people were concerned—and, as such, it seemed beyond the grasp of developers and the gentrification that had already disrupted and displaced inner urban communities in recent memory throughout the 1990s and early 2000s. But no. Make no mistake, this landscape was not a forgotten corner of Albion; it had been a manufactured landscape. However, in a couple of decades, it evolved its own logic and nature. If ever a part of the city captured a sense of liminality, it was here, and at night the edgeland qualities of the place seemed even more potent. For on Pomona Island, the entanglements of nature and artificial, body and landscape, urban and not, history and future were fused together in ways that were intoxicating. After dark, this place hums with possibility—a veritable secret pocket, its contents stashed away from the city. Standing in the tenebrous undergrowth between concrete barriers, the future city shimmers in the night, its constellation of lights slowly but steadily making their way towards and across this landscape. In their wake, the subtle murmurs and utterances of this place will be replaced by the Sturm und Drang of urban life. One of the last remnants of the compost city suddenly and sharply regenerated beyond recognition. But not yet. Right now, this endarkened isle retains its aura and provides respite, allowing the mind and body to wander its mysticality. Places like this are rapidly disappearing from cities, and accompanying this passing is a profound loss of sites for creativity and thinking.

Why should such a relatively small piece of wasteland seem so powerful? Its apparent isolation is undoubtedly part of its appeal and contributes to its outlier status. In terms of location, Pomona lies at the boundaries of three boroughs, further emphasising its character as an interzone or lost island. Arriving via the only dedicated footbridge, the site is one of defiance and turbulence. Upturned land presents an alien dunescape due to the uprooted mature trees, upon which new saplings reach to the sky. Through cracks in the concrete, moss and lichen fuzz along its hard edges and thrive. Pomona's identity as an area of ecological importance has been disturbed through several bouts of digging to try to purge it of rare plant life. In doing so, the fragments of its past twinkle in its soil as tiny ceramic reminders of the factory explosion nearly 150 years ago. Those remnants persist alongside the unloved flora, finding new ways to survive amidst the turmoil. At night, these elements coexist to shape a very different type of place that is a short distance yet worlds away from the rest of the city. The dark carpet of undergrowth and detritus requires slow and careful navigation, waving fronds of plastic and plants in the night breeze animates the undulating landscape, and the uncanny sense of futures past reverberates with each footstep. This place is rapidly disappearing under the concrete footfall of residential towers as wave after wave of regeneration alters the city. Like darkness, the wildness of such environments lies beaten and exhausted in the slivers and cracks that defy the glare of urban development.

IDEOLOGIES

PHILOSOPHIES OF THE DARK

Darkness's negative connotations are often obstacles to thinking about darkness in relation to thought. Think of it. *Darkness.* What comes to your mind? It might be that you feel at peace, immersed in a situation that gently takes away the worries of the day and replaces them with an inner calm. It could also be that you feel frightened, isolated, and vulnerable, unable to know what is surrounding you and what it might contain. The metaphorical use of light has been an enduring and popular theme in both Eastern and Western philosophies. Light has been widely associated with knowledge, clarity, and wisdom. Despite the dominance of this way of thinking, not all branches of philosophy make their way toward the light. In Chinese philosophy, Daoism offers a way that does not diminish darkness in favour of light, considering both to be equally valuable. The dao means 'the way' and refers to the natural order of the universe, its rhythms and coexistences. It is a positive philosophy that promotes a deep connection of an individual's reality with the world around them. This approach has been further illustrated through practices of Neo-Daoism, which is referred to as 'dark' learning or 'dark' understanding, *xuanxue*.[31] Of interest here is that when Daoists reach a stage where argument can no longer be pursued, they do not attempt to provide clarification but instead accept the state of ambiguity, ineffability, and obscurity that darkness presents. This ability to engage with unknowing is critical if we are to move towards a new way of understanding our world that does not seek to provide easy—albeit false—solutions to a complex, dynamic, and increasingly uncertain world.

From our origins as a species, humans have been extremely wary of darkness. Our earliest encounters with it were fraught with danger, whether from predators or hazardous landscape conditions that could not be seen. Light, therefore, quickly became deeply associated with notions of safety and security. With the discovery of fire, light also brought power, both literally, in terms of heat, and symbolically, in terms of our dominance over darkness. This latter aspect meant that humans were suddenly able to illuminate places in the world that had previously been engulfed in gloom or were considered precarious due to night. The capacity of this earliest form of artificial light to ward off peril, whether real or imaginary, soon consolidated our relationship with light and dark into one that sought the former over the latter. It quickly became understood that light at night offered protection, banishing as it did the dangers of the world. It thus also began associations of good and bad with light and dark, respectively.

While it is tempting to consider that this binary attitude towards light and dark was adopted around the globe, this is simply not true. Intricate and diverse nocturnal practices and understandings were evident in African, Arabian, Indian, Native American, Polynesian, and South American cultures. Together, these disprove the notion of any universal, overdetermined ideas about the meanings of darkness and its values. Yet, while this evidence may endure, the dominance of specific canons of thought, especially Western ones, has led to a situation where the misunderstanding of light and dark being in a binary relationship has prevailed.

As humans became more formalised in terms of their organisation and sense of civilisation, they began to develop various ideas concerning their role within the wider world and, indeed, the cosmos. These different ideas manifest themselves as religious beliefs and philosophical perspectives. Initially bound together, during the sixth century BC the separation of philosophy and science from theology began. Yet they still shared common views concerning the notion of light as representative of goodness, purity, and truth, essential to worthy pursuit. Fundamental to this framing was Plato's work in the fifth century BC. His use of light as vital to the escape from the false world of darkness, as symbolised by the cave, and into the goodness and truth of sunlight became foundational to the idea of positive transition. This perspective was enhanced by the philosophy of Cicero in the first century BC, who alloyed natural light with the notion of inner moral truth.[32] This established the internalisation of the light metaphor. This idea reached its apogee in the work of René Descartes. For example, his *Traité du monde et de la lumière* (*Treatise of the World and Light*), in which he offers a new vision of the natural world, which has continued to shape much thought since.[33] Of relevance here is his observation on the difference between our sensations and the things that produce them, that is, the natural light by which we see and how it enters our body so we can make sense of the world.

In subsequent work, Descartes uses the term 'natural light'. In his *Meditations*, natural light is the ability to recognise truth and falsehood. Natural light, here, is positioned as an internal faculty that enables this recognition, and there is nothing further, superior to the natural light, which can show that it is false. Light, as construed in this formulation, is the ultimate dimension to our understanding and making meaning of the world around us, since it cannot be called into doubt. Although Descartes had referenced natural light in some of his previous works, such as the *Discourse* and the *Rules*, its role remained ambiguous in relation to reason and therefore suggests that the term was literal. However, in the *Meditations*, the role performed by natural light is critical to the argument Descartes sets out, where it is a faculty that provides us with knowledge exempt from the machinations of the evil genius.

In Descartes's conception, natural light gives a level of certainty that is immune to doubt.

In the Enlightenment, the light metaphor resurfaces but in a very different way. Truth is not internal light but must be brought into the light so that human rationality and science can shine on it objectively. This symbolism of light is simultaneously repeated and extended in various ways throughout the history of Christianity. In such concoctions, whether they concern internal or external conflicts, philosophical inquiry, or religious creed, they all emphasise that humanity must always be led toward the light and thus enlightenment, if not salvation. In these works, we are always instructed to move from the darkness. It is deemed problematic, a place that is either morally unsafe or where ignorance resides.

Darkness worries people, representing the incomprehensible and dangerous. Western philosophers have subscribed to this way of thinking about darkness metaphorically. Therefore, they strive to get around it or through it, to alter it, ultimately to diminish its presence and influence. Light is alloyed to goodness. The flip side, of course, being that darkness is the bedfellow of danger and the unknown. It is precarious and ambiguous yet potent in its power to keep us unaware or ensnared in moral turpitude. Popular culture and religion have reinforced these ideas; we are told we must not submit to our darkest thoughts.

This influence lingers in common references made to 'dark forces', 'dark tourism', and the 'dark web', for example, wherein darkness remains synonymous with the malevolent, sinister, perverse, and backward. We can see, on many different levels, that darkness is culturally bound with negative associations. Where it is used in other terms such as 'dark matter' and 'dark energy', in astronomy and physical cosmology, it represents the unknown. However, the use of the prefix in both cases not only refers to the invisible nature of these things but also implies something mysterious, shadowy, or suspicious. Articles referring to dark energy as the 'evil' counterpart to gravity reinforce this and extend the good–bad duality of light and dark into aspects we don't even know about.[34] This is not a new idea, though, with 'dark' often deployed historically to signify the incomprehensible, the problematic, or the strange.

Despite light being the dominant metaphor for positive attributes in the West, this does not mean that darkness has been overlooked. A more positive framing of darkness is evident in the work of a range of thinkers in the Western tradition. Martin Heidegger and Jacques Derrida, for example, offer alternative understandings of light and dark's duality to overcome the dominant hierarchy of light being considered more important than darkness.[35] Both argue that what the light metaphor represents in terms of clarity and objectivity is not only impossible but also crucially undesirable. Considered in philosophical terms, darkness brings out a need to shed light on it and make something present as if it were deliberately and problematically hidden. Western philosophy is founded on the ideology of light being good. From our earliest beginnings, humans around the globe have been distrustful of darkness and have allied light with security, power, and possibility. Although light and dark were both seen as primordial principles, the hierarchical approach of preferring light above darkness was already evident in the work of pre-Socratic Greek philosopher Parmenides as far back as the fifth century BC. The notion that light should overcome darkness or at least keep it at bay has endured since in Western thought.

The 'knowing-as-seeing' metaphor appears to be an idea with widespread appeal outside Western thought, too, for example, in Indian philosophy. However, the specific dominance of light over darkness that is prevalent in the Western tradition may be particular to the metaphysics of presence that evolved in the West, where light enables presence and darkness is absence. In Chinese philosophy, the metaphor of darkness is used in specific instances to represent the goal of philosophical effort and is more important than light in Daoism. This application is evident in the two classical Daoist texts, the *Daodejing* and the *Zhuangzi*, and is also apparent in the work of Neo-Daoist philosopher Guo Xiang.

In the *Daodejing*, there are multiple uses of darkness in a positive sense where it represents being productive, profound, or deep. In this philosophy, the preference for darkness, ambiguity, and incompleteness is merged in Daoism in general with a suspicion of clarity.[36] This is because clarity, as viewed from this perspective, is understood as the false result of consideration and discrimination, which are discredited in both the *Daodejing* and the *Zhuangzi*. They avoid the pitfall of illusion concerning clarity and presence, preferring instead to engage with the nebulous and dark. Of relevance here is that darkness corresponds with absence of metaphysical philosophy, but with one crucial difference. In contrast to most metaphysics, where absence refers to the lack of something, in Daoism it is taken seriously as something on its own terms. It does not signify loss or omission. Rather, it illustrates the goal of philosophical thought, a process thinking that emphasises an equal duality of light and dark.

This balanced approach to light and dark in Daoism is evident in the writings of Zhuangzi, in which pairings of order and disorder, Heaven and Earth, light and dark are used to demonstrate the importance of interplay and harmony.[37] Such a perspective runs contrary to the Western fixation with using oppositional pairings to illustrate one as being better than the other, usually to the other's detriment. Zhuangzi celebrates the otherness that these pairings represent, each being equally important. These valuable perspectives have been somewhat buried over time, literally lost in translation. There has been a longstanding tradition of Western translators preferring not to use the word 'dark' or 'darkening' as translation for the core aspects of *ming* or *xuan*. Instead, they have employed terms such as 'deep', 'oblique', or 'profound', etc., which gives a very different reading. This is likely a hangover from the West's obsession with the light metaphor and its inability to accept darkness as positive.

The Neo-Daoist movement is also known as *xuanxue* or 'dark learning'. Two of its principal members, Wang Bi and Guo Xiang, place emphasis on darkness. The thinking of Guo Xiang, in particular, does not use darkness as a way to find metaphysical presence or transcendence. Rather than encouraging an enlightenment of the person who rises out of the world, Guo Xiang promotes the absorption of the person into the events of the world.[38] This situational shift from being detached to one of immersion is vital. Both Zhuangzi and Guo Xiang refer to the 'dark obscurity' where one is literally unable to see limits. It is here that we can detect the positive qualities that this apparent endlessness provides. By offering a realm of possibility that is away from the confines of light, darkness presents a generous and porous state of being with thought. While Heidegger and Derrida had to respond to claims that they were essentially advocating forms of negative theology, both denied this, yet this reading of their work reflects how they respectively sought to correct the metaphysical tendencies of the Western tradition. Consequently, Heidegger and Derrida remain indebted to the metaphysical tradition by trying to invert it. By contrast, Daoism was not founded on the same concepts, so it is able to demonstrate more fully how to live and navigate amongst life's rich diversity, contradictions, and complexities. This thought can unleash our imagination and creativity in new and unexpected ways. The rehabilitation of darkness, thus, presents a valuable shift in how we might navigate futures beyond existing pathways.

Adopting a philosophy like this is challenging, since it calls into question many of the supposed truths that we have accepted as conventional wisdom. To appreciate darkness, one must engage with what one immediately realises intuitively as a paradoxical entity: that darkness is where bad things thrive and also desirable, that darkness hides certain behaviours, but that things are said to emerge from the dark, that we are surprised by how our other senses are heightened when our vision is limited by darkness while also recognising its restorative qualities. What might be the purpose of doing this? In addition to the multisensory awakening that can occur within darkness, it fosters creativity and stirs the imagination. Given the challenges we now face around the world, it is timely to find new ways to think about the future. After all, darkness brings revolution. It can dissolve the prevailing hierarchies and universal myths, creating opportunity for the seditious and desirable. It is where the quiet, the secret, and the contemplative can emerge to shape the imagination and fuel the visionary. Radical thought often first stirs in the shadows.[39] The accepted conventions and established orders are suspended in the dark. Instead, alternative narratives and ways of being are ushered in with darkness.

Philosophy has been dominated by the notion of enlightenment. This tradition relies on debates of absolutism, idealism, and truth with a view to legitimise this form of thought. It is tenuously scaffolded by reason and structure to provide ordered systems of the mind. In contrast to this, there is the view that philosophy is a journey into the darkness. This embraces debates of chaos, obscurity, and contingency as a means of accounting for the mysterious and complex nature of the world. Light promises stability. Darkness offers uncertainty. Put that way, it doesn't sound like much of a choice. Yet, while the former locks us further into a specific way of thinking, the latter opens new possibilities and trajectories for how we might become. To change our perspective, we need to rethink our relationship with darkness and why we fear it.

Being afraid of the dark appears to be part of the human condition. Nearly everyone can relate to the feeling of being worried about the dark. This concern has two primary forms. Sometimes we might be frightened of some ineffable thing we perceive to be in the dark. It is the realm that enables things to be hidden from us that might, at any moment, spring forth and cause us harm. Other times we are essentially frightened of the dark itself. In this way, we simply do not know what lurks there but recognise that our lack of knowledge is the source of our fear.[40] This second form of concern is far less rational than the first. However, it is perhaps because of this ambiguity and unspeakable nature, shapelessness, that makes it so terrifying at times. Darkness is where all paths appear to intersect in terms of our fear. What if we were to go deeper into it?

Nocturnality, therefore, presents a problem. It can appear as an affront to what is human, given that we are diurnal creatures. It is easy for us to be suspicious of nocturnality; it may literally and metaphorically be seen as nonhuman. As a result, it can summon all kinds of mixed feelings within us. Night is so deeply entangled with darkness that we find it troublesome to recast our attention towards the dark in a positive way. The intention here is not to push humankind into being nocturnal but rather to subvert our expectations of the night by rethinking how we engage with it. The power of the dark needs to be reinstated as positive. Further, it must be understood as progress, a deliberate move through and beyond our obsession with light. Our relationship with artificial light has become toxic. It is harmful to human health and that of other species. Yet our attraction to it is heavily underscored by its connotations outside the technical performance of lighting.

We all form an image in our minds when prompted to think about darkness and feel it. Whether we envision a dark place, the night sky, or something else, we can all imagine it, and it is believable. But at the same time, we can also be uncertain about darkness. It is both known and unknown, palpable and intangible, seen and unseen. If we are to undo the ways in which darkness has become fused with the fearful and negative, then we need to reflect how it appears in our lives and in the world.[41] As we have seen, to justify the purity of light, darkness is often presented in a way that distorts and undermines it. Darkness is embodied in all of us, being born from it is a foundational experience of it within us. To hold darkness on its own terms rather than as an absence of light is to comprehend a richer quality of it, one that is emancipatory. Our detachment from essential darkness has produced fear. What was once a primal asset for survival now prompts us to reject anything and everything dark. Spiritual paths recognise the value of darkness as a gateway. Whether in cave dwelling, meditation places, initiations in dark forests, etc., there is a reconciliation with darkness as vital to what emerges through these inner journeys. The dark can cause distress and despair, with many people not enjoying the darkness of the night. This is completely understandable. We are frightened of what we cannot see and what we do not know. But what has been told to us about darkness has usually been twisted. The existence of darkness has been depreciated. This leads us away from our innate curiosity with it and so we resist questioning our relationship with it.

Darkness is not empty. Yet a common perception of darkness is as an absence of light. The origins of this lie with the experiments of Isaac Newton who, in the 1660s, focused his studies on the nature of colour. By using prisms to direct sunlight, he identified the colours of the rainbow that form the visible spectrum.[42] Through this work, he also concluded that darkness is an absence of light. This was an entirely new approach to looking at darkness. Up until this point, darkness had primarily been viewed as a pre-existing substance, functioning separately and adjacent to light, rather than a lack of it. Newton's work produced some significant findings but also raised a question. If darkness is an absence, then how do we experience it? This definition clearly does not account for how we encounter the dark. Most of us would be able to describe characteristics of darkness and how these make us feel. We can sense, on a fundamental level, that darkness is not simply missing light. Instead, we know it as an entity that is palpable, shifting, and despite all our attempts to capture it, unknowable. Darkness can be unsettling in this regard. It disturbs the confidence of rational thought and experience as we engage with it. It is elusive, spectral, and fleeting. Yet it is also allusive, heavy, and enduring.

DARKNESS AS PROGRESS

On 18 January 1915, six months after Europe became engulfed in the First World, Virginia Woolf wrote in her diary, 'The future is dark, which is on the whole, the best thing the future can be, I think.'[43] As Rebecca Solnit has discussed, a statement such as this is often misunderstood.[44] As a declaration, it is an assertion and celebration of the uncertainty of darkness. Here, Woolf appears to be meaning dark as in unreadable rather than dreadful. Yet the assumption of the latter is common. Or we interpret the future's opacity into something legible, a mirror for all our fears, the point at which we are unable to go beyond. Despite this tendency, time and time again throughout history we have been shown that the unfolding of events is weirder than we could have possibly imagined.

The dark is not, therefore, necessarily problematic when viewed in such a manner. Rather, it provides optimum conditions for transformation. So the binary opposition of light and dark is particularly unhelpful in thinking through the strategies of resistance and undertaking the significant changes necessary to move from how the world currently is to how it could be, were it equitable, inclusive, and sustainable. Too often, the idea of anything bad is quickly assimilated into the 'dark side', that is, it is imbued with the nefarious, untrustworthy, and problematic. However, it is also in darkness that we thrive. It is also where we might have room to breathe and create away from the glare of the always-on, always-connected tendrils of daily life. We need both light and dark.

History is made as much in the dark, indeed far more so than what necessarily is brought to light. That is, the struggles, counterpoints, common dreams, and groundswells that bring about change are not easily detected until such a transformation is about to occur, or they can only be understood with the benefit of hindsight.[45] This waiting in the wings until the moment when the performance reveals itself is pivotal to the success of revolutionary change. Too much attention too soon, and movements and motivations can become co-opted, absorbed, diffuse, or untenable through scrutiny.

It can sometimes seem difficult at this point in human history to feel positive. We might feel as if we have no plan or clear purpose. Compounding this situation is the wider sense that the world is on fire and there is nothing we can do about it.[46] Our coping mechanism for dealing with the chaos that social media hurls at us is to fall into polarising thought traps. We can quickly organise people, issues, events, and experiences into black or white folders, when in fact, all these things are far more complicated.[47] This overload is a choice. To reclaim our humanity and, by extension, our care for the living world around us, we need more creative and nuanced thinking. This sounds straightforward enough and yet it is difficult to achieve. Cultivating our innate curiosity starts with engaging with the world around us. When detached from our environment, we can quickly forget how much of the planet provides us with a sense of wonder and awe.[48] Nowhere is this perhaps more obvious than how we think about light and dark. Our fear of the dark and our ongoing obsession for a bright future are both deep-rooted and interdependent.

We instinctively move from darkness towards light in terms of how we think about the future. The former is basic, problematic, and has many negative connotations. The latter, meanwhile, suggests a clarity, openness, and brings with it associated notions of progress.

This gleaming apparition is a mirage. As with many manufactured problems, we continue in a vicious circle, committed to the idea that our ingenuity and further technological advancement will get us out of the current predicament. In truth, it is not a circle but a downward spiral. The rapid speed of development and connectivity around the globe has served to exacerbate any issues we have, transporting them far and fast. It has also led to conspicuous concealment as powerful and pervasive offshore worlds have been created.[49] Environmental degradation, loss of biodiversity, growth in non-communicable diseases, rising inequalities, and ongoing impacts of climate change now shape a new normal as far as the world is concerned.

There can be no new dawn without nightfall. To be moonstruck, unsure, and enveloped in the realm of the possible can be a gift. Recognising that the false optimism of a light-drenched future is harmful is fundamental to being able to go beyond it. With the acceleration of culture, the seemingly dematerialised and deterritorialised aspects of contemporary life can imply that we are also whizzing about, untethered, outside of time and space. Ironically, it is the situated and relational aspects of life that present the most significant opportunity for us to embrace our human condition and be creative. Drawing ourselves into the dark, we can quickly understand that alternatives are present here and now, sometimes at the flick of a switch. This pluriverse is perverse. We know that there are other futures available but find it extremely difficult to get off our business-as-usual pathways. Tackling the binary of light and dark might hold some clues for how we transition our thinking.

As evening unfolds and the spaces around us begin to gather the gloom, many of us reach for a light switch. This simple, innocuous act happens countless times around the world between dusk and dawn. Beneath it is the fact that we have mastery over the passage of darkness. Of course, we don't think about it like this. Artificial light is a matter of convenience alongside other comforts we take for granted. Yet this instant change from dark to light has unmoored us from the rhythms that had kept us attuned to the wider world. The transitions between day and night and night and day have been astonishingly consistent for millennia. Dusk and dawn have both provided reliable environmental cues for informing ecological and evolutionary processes.[50] That is until recently. Our light-saturated lives have all but obliterated dusk as we can no longer sense the approach of dark. For all its benefits, being constantly drenched in light alters how our bodies work. Undetected, light enters us, disrupting our body clocks and those of our nonhuman neighbours.

Dusk is vital. It gives us physical and psychological markers, easing the transition from day to night as darkness unfurls. It is also delicate. Light pollution produces a false non-dusk, bringing quick illumination rather than the restorative accumulation of darkness.[51] The in-betweenness of dusk enables transition and overlapping while encouraging the continuity of some things and the separation of others. This space and time also offer us the chance to move between past and future, to acknowledge things as they are in the world but also imagine how they might be. Perhaps we are getting ahead of ourselves. For before dusk, there is twilight.

Twilight is the illumination of the lower atmosphere when the sun is not directly visible, below the horizon. The phenomenon of twilight is formed by sunlight scattering in the upper atmosphere, illuminating the lower atmosphere so that the Earth's surface is neither completely lit nor completely dark. Although it is perhaps more commonly associated with evening and sunset, twilight also occurs before sunrise. This former relationship has resulted in the word *twilight* also becoming analogous to something's losing its power or approaching its end. So it is important to remind ourselves that it also represents the oncoming of a new day or rebirth. Due to its distinctive quality, primarily the absence of shadows and the appearance of objects silhouetted against the lit sky, twilight has long fascinated painters and, more recently, photographers who often refer to it as the blue hour, after the French expression *l'heure bleue*.[52] Twilight is a phenomenon that ushers in much transformation as our world appears more ambiguous or obscure. Darkness gently rises, seemingly from the ground, or sweeps across landscapes as the sun dips further and further away. It is where the mingling between the day behind us and the night before us, or vice versa, takes place. Twilight also reconfigures our more-than-human world, as nonhumans who would seldom be present during daylit hours go about their lives while many of those who are out and about in the daytime rest.

As the threshold between night and day, twilight brings an uncertain world that stimulates thought and creativity. For maybe here, in the twilight period between day and night, lies the potential for the not quite dark, not fully known, and not yet realised. This refers to the world both as perceived and as metaphor for how we might embrace the weird and eerie spaces between what is probable and what is possible. If we consider the darkness of night as a time-space across which what is visually perceived no longer equates to clarity and accuracy—a world where the imagination anticipates form rather than recognises it—then how might the descent towards it at dusk, or the ascent from it at dawn, provide the preconditions for radically rethinking our place in the world?

This movement—the shift that twilight brings—is a helpful reminder that the rhythms of day and night go on. We can perhaps feel as though darkness moves across the land, wrapping us in its inky blanket, before slowly and surely drawing itself back so that the light gets in. This is not true. It is us that is turning into the darkness of the night and through it. This darkness is caused by Earth's shadow and is always on the side farthest from the sun. Darkness, therefore, is always waiting to embrace us as Earth rotates and we move into it. But maybe we emerge from the darkness and move into the light, rotating through the cycle of planetary movement. Recognising the equal importance of light and dark is essential. Since we are diurnal beings, it is perhaps inevitable that we would prioritise the daytime and light over the night and darkness. Our preoccupation with light has relegated darkness to the margins of our thinking and lived experience. It has been diminished, derogated, and demonised. Consequently, darkness languishes in the conceptual gutter, weighed down by the slippery, negative connotations it evokes. Yet, as we have seen, there is considerable potential in embracing it to think differently. For in darkness, alternative futures await our imagination.

COMMONS

10 p.m. Double dark out here. Suburban cosmology. Roofs and the filigree of utilities dip into the ink sky. Pinpricks of celestial light deep and far away. Stepping out of the city's inner suburbs, I enter the woodland slowly. It feels like a fever dream as the chain-link fence to my right negotiates the boundary between allotments and wildness. Light leaches in from the occasional house window or streetlamp. I instinctively move further into the woods to better settle my night vision. Leaning against a fallen tree, my senses slowly acclimate to the dark. What was once a deep-grey world of unfathomable extent gently reveals itself, as different features of the wood become discernible. Feet find a gravel path and I cross the bridge over Chorlton Brook. Its soft babble flows beyond a bend and out towards the river. I follow a crooked line between more woods and meadow until I emerge at the edge of the River Mersey. Across Jackson's Boat Bridge, woodland gathers around me, the path supple with mud underfoot. The hedge and treelines give way to the tuft and tumble of a field. My boots sink into its soft, thick carpet as I approach the artificial lake beyond. This area is a flood plain and regularly becomes a series of temporary lakes in its ongoing translations between land and water. Just as the sunken land will rise again, my body shifts in its exchange with the landscape, smudging the boundaries of where one begins and the other ends.

Sale Water Park. A dark mirror ripples out in front of me. It seems to draw the surrounding landscape to it, trees and hedgerows all crouched down together in charcoal hues. Resisting this pull are the electricity pylons, defiantly striding atop the land, dull metal angles and cables stretching to infinity. The sky is awash with deep blues and yellow-grey tinges. Waterfowl splosh about by the edge of the water, sensing my presence. Although it is dark here, there is enough light to move around, to witness and be witnessed. The expanse of land renders me exposed, my human form out of kilter with the flat terrain. As I walk along the concrete jetty, my shadow twin ripples along the water before we stop to acknowledge one another.

Under the M60 motorway, the geometry shifts from fuzzy and freeform to crisp and planar. With my back to the brick wall, I am rewarded with an intimate courtship between light and dark. The sharp angles of yellow streetlamps from the motorway overhead slip through the gaps in the concrete sky, fold down its pillars, and strike across the canal's brooding surface. The deep colour of the illumination, and lack of it, seems to be almost hewn from the materials it touches, a temporary sculpture carved by place and time as infrastructures overlap. It is captivating, and I am held by wonderment. The stillness in the air is thrilling. Everything is holding its breath in anticipation as the world continues its movement through space and time. Sated by this impromptu display, it is time to move on.

Walking along the Bridgewater Way, the canal sits calmly beside me, a parallel strip of sky caught in the ground. The sandy and stony path powders my boots in response to their steps. Geese glide silently against the opposite edge of the water. Continuing along the canal towpath, I weave through the backsides of industrial estates, retail parks, and head towards the city centre. It is quiet down here. Aside from my own sounds and movements, anything else is either nonhuman neighbours or the rumblings of unseen vehicles far away. Along the canal there is an ongoing contest between that which is urban and that which is not. Corrugated metal fence panels present a hard face to the burling forms of nature opposite.

To walk along here at night is to experience a kaleidoscope of the city and the un-city as each flips and folds over the other. There is a spectrum of darkness down here. From the deep earth, dark, where I can barely see my feet, to the steel-sheet greys that hang like gauze across surfaces. Darkness is thick and fibrous, and I can almost feel its weight in my hand. Darkness is also gossamer and fleeting, diffusing like mist as I approach. In between these extremes are countless collaborations between dark and light. These coexistences are the basis of everything. Without them, we simply cannot be. Even in the manufactured landscape of a city, there is a need for darkness.

As I follow the canal towpath towards the city, the urban fabric affirms its presence. Blocks and blocks of apartments huddle into view. The odd window is illuminated, but most people are asleep. Light bobbles on the water and the hum of traffic builds. As the artificial light grows around me, deep pockets of shadow become scarce within the white-yellow-grey fuzz of the urban environment. Castlefield shares its industrial matrix of viaducts and waterways. Huge, silent testaments to the past formed in Victorian steel and brick. In a couple of hours, trams and trains will snake their way along the active lines while the third lies dormant to transport, offering itself as a temporary sky garden. The replacement of sodium lamps with white LEDs in the late 2010s has completely changed the atmosphere of this area after dark. Like other parts of the city, the nocturnal ambiances and some of the nuances of shadow play that shaped the identity of this place have been lost. This version of the city leaches artificial light everywhere at night, not least into the sky.

The choreography of Manchester at night, as with other cities, needs to progress towards a range of coexistences of light and dark that supports a vibrant city full of contrasts and experiences. Having been here many times before between dusk and dawn, I can just about remember how the washes and tones of previously installed light accentuated the industrial structures and created an enchanting urban area. Yet as the city sleeps, its brightness continues apace. I then find a small oasis of darkness smuggled under the overlapping shadows of an arch. Carefully, I inhabit it and close my eyes. With my body at rest, my mind reflects and begins to reimagine the city, its residents waking up to a revitalised Manchester celebrating its nocturnal hours in ways that are inclusive of people and other beings. This new city supports conviviality while recognising the need for intergenerational life to flourish. Safe and inclusive, this city after dark brings people together to share in the nocturnal commons and to wonder at the star-filled sky. Reconnecting with the global heritage of dark skies, they recognise the ways in which everyone and everything is connected in a beautiful yet fragile way. Far from exhausting ourselves in the pursuit of being always-on and dragging the day into the night, this city's population knows that a life of light alone is a life half lived. We need light and dark in balance.

The hydraulic groan of a waste disposal truck snaps me out of this reverie. Moisture thickens the air and begins to glisten on the surfaces of the city. The urban landscape sparkles with tiny galaxies that only reinforce the lack of visibility of the one above the planet. The city is starting to stir, its pulse steadily increasing as it emerges from slumber. Turning my back on the city centre, the new towers around Great Jackson Street soar to the sky, gleaming and spiralling upward. The city is always a process and in flux, but these new additions seem uncertain of their role and, despite their size, give little back. Instead, they are curiously flat, an implication of a dense urban skyline without the substance to share with the streets below. As a backdrop for the city after dark, such architecture has a basic scenographic function. But is this all we can hope for and desire the nocturnal city?

ECOLOGIES

LIFE AFTER DARK

As evening beckons, many of us head back home and begin our transition from day to night. Meals are prepared, care and other forms of domestic labour are undertaken. As we engage in these activities, we usually withdraw from the rhythms and routines of the daytime. Insulated from the outside world, we are less attuned to what is going on out there, our awareness of its flora and fauna restricted to what we can see through the windows and glazed doors of our homes. As twilight unfolds, in most situations we have already put lights on to carry on with whatever we are doing. We may even draw the curtains or lower the blinds before nightfall. We flick more switches, turn on devices, and tap apps to bring forth more artificial light into the dark following day's close.

Outside, however, the natural world does not stop. We may remove ourselves from the outdoor environment, yet on it lives. Our lives carry a characteristically different sense of purpose, and this has encouraged us to view the world with human values, overlooking the qualities of place that enable the flourishing of other species in different ways.[53] Above, around, and underneath our homes, there is considerable life after dark. It also carries on, living on the surfaces and in the nooks and crannies of our homes, of course, out of view or undetectable by human eyes. Life after dark is a multiscalar phenomenon. It teems across our lands, oceans, and skies, or lies dormant in the permafrost, biding its time. In all its permutations, the collective life of this planet is astonishing. Yet we human beings have not always respected and protected the other species we share our world with. Beyond deliberate acts of environmental destruction and degradation, we cause harm and even existential threat to nonhuman life without realising it. A good example is the impact that light pollution has.

Artificial light at night has revolutionised the way we live and work, but it has also come with various costs. When used carelessly, lighting disrupts wildlife, damages human health, wastes money and energy, contributes to climate change, and blocks our view of the starry sky. Why does this matter? In 2001, Pierantonio Cinzano and his colleagues produced the first global atlas of light pollution.[54] They calculated that two-thirds of the world's population lived in areas with light pollution, meaning that nights were at least 10 per cent brighter than natural darkness. The scale of the global problem of light pollution was only revealed when the team updated their atlas in 2016. At that point, it was identified that 83 per cent of people around the world lived under a light-polluted sky, and in the UK, Europe, and North America, the figure was even higher, at 99 per cent.[55] More recent research conducted in 2021 has shown that there has been an acceleration of light pollution around the world by 270 per cent globally and up to 400 per cent in some regions.[56] Light is everywhere. While it is vital to the rhythms of life, too much of it in the wrong place or at the wrong time causes big problems. Restoring darkness can help mitigate some of these issues and support better stewardship of the planet we share.

Before we get into the specific issues that excessive artificial light causes, let us first zoom out for a moment and think about how environmental issues are widely perceived. Climate change, as with other environmental matters, is generally considered a phenomenon that occurs during the daytime. Perhaps this is because it is when we, as diurnal creatures, mainly witness its effects. We literally see what is happening though often only at the point of which a substantial change becomes evident, which is usually the result of a longer, more discreet process or series of cascading effects. We see the emaciated wraith of the polar bear on dwindling ice as a powerful image that seems to encapsulate the damage we are doing to the environment and the countless other species that depend on it. Now, let's think about the night. Do biodiversity loss, ecosystem disruption, environmental degradation, extreme weather events, and climate change happen after dark? They do.

In fact, global warming is heating up nights more quickly than days, with profound effects on other species. Throughout most of the world and over the span of thirty-five years to 2017, the average temperature increase at night has outpaced those of the daytime.[57] Since different animals and plants carry out different activities and processes in relation to the time of day, unequal temperature rises may have a skewed impact. Ecosystems are delicately balanced, so variations in temperature and precipitation can have significant consequences for the species inhabiting these regions and their ability to adapt. For example, greater warming at night is associated with the climate becoming wetter, which has major ramifications for plant growth and how species such as insects and mammals interact. The difficulty is that we are not often present to witness these changes and realise what is occurring amongst all the precious life after dark.

Over time, we have become further and further removed from the world around us. One consequence of this is evident in how we think about and illustrate the natural world. Ecocriticism is often assumed to be 'green'.[58] The origin of this assumption has been an association of ecology and, by extension, ecocriticism, with pastoral and romantic depictions of certain kinds of nature that speak of the unspoilt, distant, and revered forests and meadows. By contrast, those places where anthropogenic activity has altered their nature, such as cityscapes, farm factories, and urban rivers, are not readily accounted for. This basis, which has positioned humans as separate from the rest of nature, is quite rightly being challenged from several directions. Of relevance here is the insistence on a significantly more diverse, less pretty, and distinctly darker view of ecology and its representations.[59] This dark turn, in all its forms, is explicitly anti-anthropocentric, a stance that aligns it with another turn in the humanities and social sciences—the *animal turn*, which seeks to provide wider and deeper descriptions than are possible with a humancentric view.

Eco-philosopher Timothy Morton has argued for the inclusion of 'dark ecology' in our thinking about nature. Rather than trying to ignore the paradoxes that exist within nature, this approach accepts it is contingent and queer. Dark ecology, he proposes, puts hesitation, uncertainty, irony, and thoughtfulness back into ecological thinking.[60] It does not attempt to tidy up nature towards an impossible pristine state but instead revels in its negativity, ugliness, and horror. By embracing a vision of nature's darker side, such work seeks to create a fuller understanding of humanity's relation to nature. This approach aligns with the alternative ideologies and philosophies discussed in this book's previous section by encouraging us to acknowledge the provisional, ambiguous, and troubling qualities of the world around us. While it is valuable to think through the dark ecology or dark turn in the wider sense of ecocriticism, it is also important not to underestimate its role in contributing to a change in how we view darkness in a positive sense. Here, the dark represents the complex, ineffable and thus essential aspects of our wider world. By the same token, there is increasing evidence of how serious the non-visual effects of light can be for us and, indeed, other species. We might think of this change in planetary conditions as the loss of night.

THE LOSS OF NIGHT

Darkness is integral to biodiversity. For billions of years, all life has depended upon Earth's rhythm of day and night. This predictable pattern has been embedded in the DNA of all animals and plants. They rely on this cycle of light and dark to inform their behaviours, since it tells them when to eat, reproduce, and sleep, and provides them protection from predators. Humans have disrupted this cycle through their use of artificial light at night.[61] The growing body of scientific evidence shows that this artificial light is having negative and deadly impacts on many different types of *life forms*, including amphibians, birds, insects, mammals, and plants.[62] Darkness is vital to life everywhere. Its reduction through light pollution is having serious effects, yet because we still do not know the full implications of these impacts, alterations in the nocturnal behaviours and rhythms of flora and fauna inscribe themselves largely undetected.

Despite the ongoing expansion of illumination into previously unlit realms, such as rural areas, while technologies of lighting extend around the world, the distribution of darkness and light often remains geographically and culturally specific. Around the world, there are still some deserts, caves, and deep-sea trenches that remain bereft of light, but all other territories have to some extent been invaded by light pollution or are in constant threat of its encroachment. Defending darkness across space has been most diligently championed by DarkSky, formerly the International Dark-Sky Association (IDA).[63] This has led to an expanding global network of designated International Dark-Sky communities, parks, reserves, and sanctuaries managing to safeguard dark skies and nocturnal habitats through minimising light pollution. To promote their mission and values within urban environments as effectively as possible, DarkSky has an additional category, Urban Night Sky Places, whose design and planning actively support an authentic nighttime experience amid significant artificial light. Such preservation is critical. Yet the overriding desire for artificial illumination in urban landscapes has resulted in a polarisation of bright cities and towns versus dark rural places, with the latter often trying to resist the increasing threat of light pollution from the former.

We need to be clear: too much light in the wrong place or at the wrong time causes havoc. It radically alters the way living things behave. Until recently, the production of artificial light at night was limited to Earth. However, in the race for space as the final frontier of profit, magnates and entrepreneurs are altering the situation above Earth's atmosphere, too. Space has rapidly become the last commons to be exploited through various claims and attempts to colonise it.[64] This uninhibited expansion has neither been accountable to governments nor answerable to communities all around the world. Access to space used to be restricted to state governments or international agencies for collaboration as they had the knowledge, infrastructure, and resources to facilitate space exploration. Beginning in 2018, however, 30,000 low-altitude satellites were sent into space by SpaceX. In addition to the ceaseless radio signals that were now being rained down upon the world, the rapid pollution of the night sky took astronomers by surprise.[65] From 2019 onward, the night sky has become congested with hundreds, then thousands, of internet satellites, and these fake stars may soon outnumber real ones if this trend continues.[66]

It might seem a moot point to raise this new source of light pollution as a problem when we already have a lot to deal with that is terrestrial. Also, perhaps it is rather inconsequential given that most of us live under the yellow-grey blanket of light pollution. There is a major difference. Unlike the excessive lighting that is fixed to the manufactured infrastructures built around the world, the fast-moving satellites are able to penetrate parts of the planet that were previously remote enough not be affected. For those last Indigenous communities that still have an intimate relationship with the sky at night, the presence of these artificial stars will be immediate and detrimental. Rather than pursue these exploits of space colonisation, we need to become better stewards of the planet for the benefit of collective life and its future generations. Ensuring those that follow us can flourish on a hospitable and biodiverse planet is essential. Reconnecting us all to the nocturnal commons of starry skies at night is part of the journey towards this goal.

The ongoing impacts of the Anthropocene—a geological era defined by the actions of humans, specifically in the form of a globalised system of capital accumulation through resource extraction—has initiated what some refer to as the sixth mass extinction event. In contrast to the previous extinction events caused by natural phenomena, this one is driven by human activity. It primarily relates to the unsustainable use of land, water, and energy, and climate change. Amongst this worrying stack of ecological impacts is one that has been given little attention—sensory pollution. By radically changing the world to prioritise an economic system, we have profoundly altered the sensory worlds of other species.[67] The onslaught of artificial stimuli has created noise where there was quiet, put toxic molecules into water and soil, and caused the night to be filled with light. Disturbing the sensory worlds of these creatures has consequences that are hard to predict. Artificial light, for example, reconfigures the more-than-human communities around them, attracting some and repelling others. By overpowering the stimuli that connect animals to each other and their environment, sensory pollution not only detaches us from the wider ecosystems but also enforces this disconnection onto other species. Preserving darkness and other environmental attributes to help restore sensory lifeworlds of all living things is imperative if we wish to safeguard biodiversity.

As we already have encountered, light is often considered synonymous with knowledge, goodness, progress, safety, and security. Darkness, through its denigration in relation to light, has come to represent ignorance, evil, stagnation, danger, and uncertainty. The human obsession with bringing more and more light into our lives makes it feel like an affront to think of it as something that pollutes our world. Yet when we put it in places and times where it doesn't belong, then that is exactly what it is. In this context, a consideration about darkness and the unequal and often excessive use of light, and the values, meanings, and feelings that surround them, is usefully framed by Jacques Rancière, who explains how both sensory experience and making sense are inherently political. He argues that such regimes of the sensible are shaped by specific values espoused by the powerful, who configure environments as common sensical realms that are difficult to imagine otherwise.[68] With most of us living under light-polluted skies, it is not surprising that most of us do not know what darkness really is. Without this experience, cascading impacts emerge that become increasingly difficult to stop. This is because we begin to normalise the destruction of lifeworlds that are entirely reliant on the coexistence of light and dark. Even bleaker, as we grow desensitised to this situation, we are less likely to do anything to change it. This is not simply a matter of avoiding an extinction of experience; it concerns the eradication of many species. Awareness is only the beginning. We need to act. But we generally don't.

Perhaps the difficulty where life between dusk and dawn is concerned is one of perception. We struggle with the dark and nocturnal aspects of the world. Associations with nocturnality are often more-than-human or even inhuman. Religious beliefs and folktales concerning human-beast hybrids, the undead, the vampiric, and the supernatural beings that claim the cloak of darkness for their wrongdoings have endured. Such ideas appear to be transgressive to all that is human. As a result, we have ended up in a situation where darkness seems unnatural to us or, at best, something to be wary of. To embrace nocturnality is not to suggest we need to live outside ourselves but rather to reconnect with what it means to be human and the rhythms of life that we have disconnected from. Instead, we need more empathy and closeness with our world and the many different forms of life we share it with, and this does not pertain solely to the daytime. But the desire to banish the nocturnal and stretch the diurnal world endures despite its consequences. Perhaps it is toward the crepuscular that we should pay more attention for clues to how to manage this transition.

A crepuscular animal is active primarily during the twilight period, being matutinal, vespertine, or both. This has much to do with available light, so these boundaries are not necessarily as firm as they may first appear. For example, some crepuscular animals might also be active under moonlight or during an overcast day. Matutinal animals are active only before sunrise, while vespertine animals are active only after sunset. Although a series of factors influence the time of day an animal is active, there has been an increasing shift of animals becoming more nocturnal to avoid humans.[69] We are pushing others into the dark. Once they are there, they too become all but invisible to us—out of sight and out of mind—meaning that their existence is more precarious, since they can easily slip out of our worldviews. With the loss of night comes the loss of countless species.

Strategies and designs for responsible lighting might embrace different ways of phasing levels of artificial light in terms of quantity and quality, carefully considering the most appropriate colour temperature and the number of lumens to cause minimal disruption to our more-than-human world. This would enable the manufactured world to at least be more attuned to the planetary rhythms of light and dark, affording all creatures—including humans—to navigate dusk and dawn in a more natural way, with all the benefits and nuances that it provides as part of a healthy, biodiverse ecosystem. The periods of transition that twilight represent provide important physical and emotional markers.

Rather than literally flicking a switch between that which is gathering dark and bright light, a far less abrupt shift would reconnect us to the collective life of the planet. This seems a simple and sensible thing to do. A major obstacle in achieving this goal is that we have largely become accustomed to levels of light that would have been unimaginable to our ancestors. It is challenging to recognise how much darker nights once were, even during our own lifetimes, due to light pollution's increase and spread. Given the destructive environmental effects resulting from the ongoing expansion of illumination across dark spaces, new thinking amongst policy-makers, environmentalists, technologists, and lighting designers is crucial. Our knowledge of the impact we are having as a species on the planet grows, yet we are in danger of losing connection with the very source of darkness that has been with us since we first evolved and, indeed, long before then.

BROKEN RHYTHMS

Dark skies are essential to the rhythms of life on Earth, with the evolution of different species originating from the planet's rotation around its axis as it orbits the sun. Amidst the current era of ecological crisis, it is easy to overlook the need for natural darkness. In comparison to climate change, acid rain, loss of exotic species, and habitat destruction, it can appear less urgent and important. This, however, underestimates the role of light and dark's rhythms supporting Earth in three significant ways. First, they enable the primary productivity of food webs, producing oxygen and regulating carbon cycling and sequestration. Second, they foster more and greater diversity of interactions between species. Third, they help ensure the resilience of ecosystems. The essential role of rhythms of light and dark in shaping daily, monthly, and seasonal cycles is disrupted by artificial light at night. Artificial light has been linked to impacts on our health and psychological well-being, our built environment, and the wider world.[70]

Altering natural cycles of light and dark directly affects the rhythms of our bodies and minds, with profound health consequences evident in a growing body of scientific research. As the percentage of night work, long hours, and on-call work increases in countries around the globe, so do the health risks of sleep and circadian disruptions. These include cancer, cardiovascular disease, diabetes, hypertension, and obesity.[71] It can also lead to insomnia and depression, both associated with the physiological health conditions stated above. Artificial light is making us less healthy than ever.[72] It can also disproportionately impact different ethnic and racial groups, adding to the already significant list of urban inequalities.[73] Is a brighter world a better world? There certainly seem to be limits to how much light we need in our lives. Yet artificial light is everywhere, an often unbidden by-product of contemporary lives. It shines from the devices we use and through the environments we inhabit. Worse, many of us do not have a choice as the changing demands of work patterns put us under the glare of artificial illumination. Both the quantity and the quality of this light have fundamentally altered, impacting the health of our species and of many others.[74] Despite this rapid growth and transformation, we still do not understand the consequences. Artificial light may be increasingly bright, white, and universal, but what of darkness?

Far from a uniform phenomenon, darkness is multiple, situational, and contested. However, even in contemporary times, in which darkness has largely been banished from the city through the expansion of social and economic activity and the resultant spread of illumination, it remains commonly perceived as intrinsic to danger. This latter point is influenced by various subjectivities such as gender, ethnicity, and age. Light, by contrast, affords visibility and disarms visibility outside areas of bright illumination; darkness thus remains enmeshed with the fearful and dangerous. Yet this implies consistent states of light and dark, each of which is subject to changing levels. Different levels of light, characterised by the depth of field and brightness, continuously play across the spaces in which we see things and with which we continually adjust, and this also applies to depths and densities of darkness. This distribution of light and dark across space is shaped by weather and seasonal patterns, diurnal temporalities, longitudinal and latitudinal positions, and the presence of cloud and atmospheric particles. Likewise, our perceptual experience of night is conditioned by the affordances of place, how moonlight shines on distinctive surfaces or reflects on water, the form of silhouettes against the starry sky, and the masses that block light.

The circadian cycle is not 24 hours; therefore, it constantly needs the signals initiated by light to match it to the human. Researchers have found that internal biological time is the most reliable predictor of peak performance time, and it is different for different people. Late in the evening, melatonin secretion begins. This hormone is produced in the brain at night. It signals the time of day and is essentially the drug that triggers sleep. Exposure to light suppresses the production of melatonin. Insufficient light, or light at the wrong time, can decouple our rhythms and disrupt our circadian rhythm. Jet lag is a good example of this, while lack of light can also contribute to Seasonal Affective Disorder. Sleeplessness can result in significantly impaired performance and, in turn, lead to accidents that may be fatal. In addition, prolonged periods of sleeplessness can make the body slowly shut down to preserve its vital functions. Ensuring we have good access to daylight is evidently beneficial for us, but the pleas for darkness appear to be missing.[75] This is not nostalgia to return to an earlier form of life or to a more primitive technology but rather an urgent appeal to find a more balanced way of living collectively on the planet.

Humans are diurnal. We sleep at night and are active during the day. At least that is the theory based on our biology, though in practice, we know that an increasing proportion of people are working at night either through long hours, on-call responsibilities, or shift work. Compared to most mammals, however, this makes us different. Most mammals do not share our predilection for daylight, since only a fifth of mammal species are diurnal like us. By contrast, nearly seventy per cent of our mammalian relatives are nocturnal. The rest are either *crepuscular*, active at dawn and dusk, or *cathemeral*, active during both day and night. Unfortunately, these behaviour patterns are increasingly disrupted by human activity. As people encroach upon animal habitats, more and more wild creatures are seeking refuge at night. To avoid interaction with humans, many different species of mammals are moving their activity from the day into the dark hours of the night. This is because numerous species have already become limited to the geographical margins of their local habitats. As a result, they are separating themselves from humans in time rather than in space. These changes are not without consequences. When so many species shift their natural patterns of behaviour, predator–prey dynamics that have evolved over generations become disturbed, which leads to unknown and potentially cascading effects on the environment.

This shift has been the subject of recent research but points towards a much wider issue. Through the ongoing processes of colonising the night, humans bring with them all manner of technologies to enable them to help overcome the limits of their diurnal selves. The capacity of our species to inhabit the night is aided and abetted by various technologies. Most obviously, perhaps, is that of artificial illumination. But this is only one element of our expansion across territory around the world. The development of settlements through subsequent civilisations during the last 6000 years has also enabled humankind to flourish. This success has been supported by a greater degree of resource extraction, construction of places to live and work, infrastructures to connect them, and increased supplies to sustain them, let alone enable further growth. The industrialisation of most dimensions of human activity, whether through farming, energy production, transportation, manufacture, or commerce, has profoundly altered the planet. Attending these enormous changes has been artificial light and its ability to maintain many of these activities around the clock or provide daytime environments where sunlight is no longer necessary because it can be reproduced. The speed and scale of the change has left significant environmental degradation, biodiversity loss, and huge amounts of different forms of pollution in its wake. Understanding how human activities are reshaping the habitats and behaviours of other species will enable us to identify pathways for coexistence.

This transformation does not just affect mammals. It is also having serious impacts on populations of amphibians, birds, fish, and reptiles. That is if we consider only vertebrates. In addition, many invertebrates are negatively impacted, including insects, snails, spiders, and worms plus many sea creatures such as anemones, coral, crabs, jellyfish, squid, and starfish.[76] That so much of these disturbances goes undetected until their impacts are significant or worse, irreversible, is hugely problematic. It is easy to ignore, even to be completely unaware of, the various comings and goings of other species, especially at night, when we generally shut ourselves off from the world. Therefore, if we are not even aware of the impact of our daytime invasions into the habitats and behaviours of other species, we are far less likely to be conscious of them at night.

Nocturnal migrations are very common. It is estimated that two-thirds of all migratory birds make their long-haul journeys at night. Night-travelling birds fly high when the moon shines in a clear sky and the stars can be seen. On cloudy nights, rain and fog result in the birds flying lower. When this happens, there is a significant risk that the large flocks can be disoriented by lights and buildings, sometimes fatally, and there are many recorded instances of birds that have collided in large numbers with manufactured structures such as lighthouses, masts, and towers.[77] It is perhaps no surprise, then, that the dazzling spectacle of cities at night is a huge disruptor to birds. High profile cases, such as the effect of the *Tribute in Light* art installation commemorating where the Twin Towers once stood, have received a lot of attention in the press. However, given how cities around the world are growing and spreading their light further and further into the surrounding landscape and higher into the atmosphere, the nights are less and less suitable for nocturnal navigation for multiple species.[78]

The ecological impact of artificial light at night on the behaviours, physiologies, and ecosystems of nonhumans has been well documented. Yet the extent to which light pollution alters plant phenology and the corresponding effect on herbivores is less clear, although there seems to be a correlation. Trees need darkness, too.[79] Plants capture sunlight by using chlorophyll, a pigment found in plant cells. As the seasons change, the colour of leaves alters from light green in the spring, through darker green in the summer and then to the range of colours we see in autumn, as the chlorophyll disappears before the leaves are eventually shed. The glow of lights, however, can deceive the organism, with leaves remaining on trees until late autumn.

As we can see, the harmful relationship between the presence of light at night with changes in development, growth, and survival in nonhuman lives, alongside the array of health consequences that affect all animals, including humans, such as increased risk of disease, weakened immune function, decreased fertility, disrupted sleep, weight gain, and (in humans) impaired mental health. The broken rhythms of light and dark evidently have profound consequences for everyone and everything. Restoring and redistributing darkness where it needs to be is paramount and would contribute significantly to the wider challenge of the climate crisis. Aside from direct benefits in supporting biodiversity, ecosystems, and, indeed, human health, it would reconnect us with the world we have become detached from.

KIN

8 p.m. After dark, urban natures are almost invisible. A few steps in any direction, however, and the traces of multispecies life in the nocturnal city become gently revealed. In established and protected sites, it is perhaps no surprise to encounter nonhuman bodies at night. But what of those places that are underrepresented and subject to turbulence? Looking away from the city centre, I step down into Corporation Street, which silently changes into Dantzic Street. Passing beneath the railway lines, I am taken to a different city, one whose nature is not only porous and contingent but also tricky and surreptitious. Standing at the beginning of the Irk Valley, its ongoing regeneration has been pounding its way across the landscape in concrete boots.

My shadow follows a brick wall which suddenly stops at a small bridge as the street branches into Collyhurst Road and Dalton Street. Over the bridge, St Catherine's Wood tumbles down to the bank of the River Irk. My feet soon become entangled in its tenebrous embrace. Overgrown, strewn with litter, unmanaged coppices, burnt-out vehicles, and many other things in between, this is a place for the abandoned and forgotten. The land yields as I climb up the slope and into the wood. At the same time, my body submits to its gloom and gradient. The isolation that one feels in these places, especially at night, is pronounced. Activity after dark around this stretch of the valley is typically not human. Unkempt and unremarkable to the casual eye, after sunset this site is otherworldly. It is a perfect place for creativity and imagination to unfurl, since the environment appears to be in a continual process of disarray and becoming rather than being ordered or finished. It also brings me face to face with many other forms of life, reminding me of the artifice of cities.

Such thresholds of urban nature make them ideal spaces in which we can think about the future. This perspective is, of course, a human one. For there are already many different species crawling, flying, scurrying, and swimming within and through the Irk Valley. Far from being a site with protected status, the large amount of detritus has two obvious benefits. It discourages human activity by inhibiting access or making it hazardous, providing a liminal zone for the more-than-human world. In addition, it provides further micro-sites of refuge for other species. In this way, these accidental buffer areas provide a valuable if barely detectable feature of these places. Back on the bridge over the River Irk as I look to the city, common pipistrelle bats arc and swoop in velvet flourishes against the navy sky.

Down by the waterside, a rat takes a casual wander atop half a dozen loose bricks. It stops, sniffs, then disappears into the shadowy fingers of overhanging plants. I turn around 180° to witness Canada geese silently paddling along the crescent of the river as it curves out of view. A cloud of moths fluttering around a streetlamp like a halo stops me in my tracks. Tiny wings of dust-brown joined in a pulsating clamour. Onwards. As I stride along Collyhurst Road again, each long step is like an incantation to the landscape, which rises swiftly on either side in response. I am not alone in this darkened topography. By Vauxhall Street, the quickstep of a young fox softly pads up the sharp incline of the former spoil heap.

Moving towards the river, perimeter fencing blocks access to the other end of St Catherine's Wood, a barcode of metal and not. This latest addition to the filigree of the land makes passage for the nightwalker harder, who must circumvent by squeezing around it by the water on a muddy bank. There are no such hindrances for the toing and froing of nocturnal kin, whose journeys are not in the least compromised by the metallic grille as they move above, between, and under it. A towering conifer breaks the skyline with its feathery branches. Slinking away from the industrial units, the road splits once more, asphalt tributaries running from the inner-urban core. Lichen and moss share their psychedelic, verdant swirls on the brick lining of a bridge. They glisten in their damp reverie, lost in the slow time of a different patina of life. Their undulating carpets are vertical gardens in miniature. Leaning beside them to look sideways, the different layers are mesmerising. The low hum of the city behind is a tender reminder that I am not far from urban life yet standing against this wall and its countless organisms could be another world. The steep incline of the main road bolts upwards to my right, but it is Smedley Road to my left which draws my gait, welcoming me down its slope. Along here, the present is uncoordinated and the future bulges out wherever it can.

Bedraggled clumps of hastily discarded waste underscore the route as household and trade debris burst forth from swollen hoarding, fences, and brick walls, spewing onto the pavement. The quietness is palpable. Resting by a slumped board, rodent neighbours scritch and scratch their way amongst cardboard before a speeding car lights up the scene with its headlights and leaves silence in its wake. Leaving the pavement behind me as it curls up towards the housing estate framed by the viaduct, a narrow asphalt path bends between trees and bushes. I weave slowly and carefully between the shrubs and copse as I veer from the smooth path and head towards the river. My boots slip-stop their way down the bank. I move inelegantly near the gurgle and splosh of water echoing from underneath the adjacent brick bridge. It is dark down here.

Trees, bushes, and grasses conspire together, rendering my progress through and around them to be a gradual if not always graceful choreography. An intermittent buzz orbits around me followed by the sensation of tiny insects about my face. My proprioception is off-kilter and unreliable amid this dark and strange place, so I focus on staying still, all the better to share the more-than-human utterances and manoeuvres of the night. I steadily ascend back up the bank, the flora caressing and tripping me in equal measure. As I turn right onto the pavement, the arches of the railway stretch away on both sides. As I pass through this portal, suburbia quietly builds itself into view. The smooth baize of a playing field is a shock after the teeming wildscapes I had been immersed in for the last couple of hours. Climbing uphill, homes seem to gather with each step as the built environment reasserts itself again. Traffic streaks across at the top of the hill, mainlining a major artery into and out of the city. The wildness shrinks back both in the landscape and within me.

TECHNOLOGIES

THE BRILLIANCE OF CITIES

Where do our ideas for collective life come from? Ever since we found the many benefits of living together in settlements, humankind has sought to evolve different forms of organisation and cohabitation. Accompanying our history of civilisation is a parallel history of cities and, indeed, different ways of envisioning collective futures. Designed cities have been traced back to the third millennium BC across Minoan, Mesopotamian, Harrapan, and Egyptian civilisations. Ideas for imaginary cities, meanwhile, follow an arc from Plato's Atlantis, circa 360 BC, through Thomas More's Utopia of 1516 to the contemporary visions made to examine and suggest how we might live together. Many of these visions are fictional, using imaginary cities of the past or future to explore narratives around the protagonist's good or ill fortune. While these fictional cities do not exist in the same way as the material facts of constructed cities around the world do, they can be highly influential in how we think urban life was or might become.[80] In the present, such visions tend to favour either optimism, alloying technology for the betterment of society, or pessimism, wherein undisclosed forms of ecocide have occurred.[81] This heaven or hell, utopian or dystopian bifurcation runs deep in the canon of visions for cities.

Imagining positive alternatives appears to be problematic, not least because the scenarios can easily be switched into technologically driven nightmares, where humanity is subservient or eking out an existence outside the gaze of machines and artificial intelligence or into green and blue untainted environments imbued with characteristics that imply freshness, abundance, energy, health, safety, and even spirituality.

Of relevance to us here are the visions produced for future cities to see whether we might be able to find hints at how urban life will become. Specifically, it is worth delving into these future visions and looking at them from how they frame light and darkness. Many urban futures, especially those within the broad and somewhat ambiguous Smart City remit, portray seemingly frictionless environments in which life is clean, coherent, and light.[82] By contrast, where it does exist, darkness is symbolic of all that is feared in a city—unseen or partially hidden dangers, dank and dirty places that appear to be the breeding ground for disease, and other forms of undesirable aspects. How did we arrive at this point where if an urban landscape is not burnished with light, it must be troubling, even threatening? Although the preservation and conservation of natural darkness is essential, urban areas currently produce huge amounts of light pollution. If we can reimagine and reconfigure the relationship between darkness and cities, we could make a big difference in tackling the impacts that artificial light at night can have. To achieve this, we need to unpack the apparent menace of darkness in visions for urban futures. Before that, however, it is worth understanding the context for how the relationship with darkness in cities has evolved over time.

Cities initially grew from a need for commerce, culture, and politics to come together efficiently. They also were places that could be governed and defended. The protection of the city came with certain obligations; these might be monetary, religious, social, or other transactions that supported those in power and contributed towards the common good. As cities grew, their boundaries went far beyond the initial fortified core or sprang up in new locations.

Life inside the city could often be viewed as beneficial but was not without its problems. This led to the emergence of watchmen: organised groups of men, usually authorised by a city, state, government, or society. Watchmen sought to deter criminal activity and provide law enforcement. In addition, they would perform the services of public safety, crime prevention and detection, fire watch, and recovery of stolen goods. Watchmen have existed since earliest recorded times in different guises around the world, generally succeeded by the development of formally organised policing.

Night presented a different set of conditions for the watchmen.[83] Streets in many cities, including major ones, were usually dark and had a shortage of artificial light. Where artificial light was present, it was often of poor quality. For centuries, it had been recognised that the onset of darkness in the unlit streets of a town heightened the threat of danger. Darkness was the domain of irrational fears but also of real hazards. It offered a refuge for the superstitious and supernatural associations it engendered. It also provided cover for the disorderly, immoral, and dangerous. These anxieties led to rules about who could use the streets after nightfall and the formation of a night watch in the thirteenth century in various countries including Denmark and England. Such rules had been long established in major cities by the curfew, after which the gates were closed and the streets cleared. Only people with good reason were permitted to travel through the city. Anyone else was deemed suspicious and potentially criminal.

The watchmen patrolled the streets after dark, calling out the hour, looking out for fires, checking that doors were locked, and delivering drunks and vagrants to the watch constable. Low wages and the uncongenial nature of the work tended to appeal only to a relatively low standard of person who, as a result, had a reputation for being ineffective and even complicit in some of the various nocturnal dealings they were supposed to prohibit. Many major cities had a system of night policing in place by the middle of the seventeenth century, though these were improved through better administration, finances, salaries, and not least, an increase in lighting. The addition of improved forms of artificial illumination that could provide more consistent and brighter sources of light such as gaslighting and, subsequently, electric lighting would transform the power of authorities to monitor and observe populations.[84]

We have a long history of artificial lighting. Originally developed out of primal need, subsequent innovations in technology have enabled us to light parts of the world in novel ways and in an increasingly uniform and brighter manner.[85] Essentially, our ingenuity in casting out darkness can be summarised as follows:

400,000 BC Woodfire
13,000 BC Grease
3000 BC Rushlight
1500 BC Oil Lamp
100 AD Tallow Candle
1780 Hollow Wick
1792 Gas Lighting
1802 Arc Lamp
1838 Lightbulb
1853 Kerosene Lamp
1860 Electric Lighthouse
1861 Photographic Flash
1868 Yablochkov Candle
1879 Street Lighting
1880 Moon Tower
1900 Neon
1901 Mercury Vapor
1925 Television
1935 Night Vision
1960 Laser
1962 LED
1964 Liquid Crystal Display
1970 Fibre Optic
1987 OLED
2013 Hydrogen Fusion

Artificial lighting was increasingly implemented in cities and towns during the eighteenth and nineteenth centuries as it became more reliable and practical to install. After the initial shock of its glare, people became accustomed to it. This meant that darkness was more deeply perceived as problematic. Darkness within interiors made cleaning difficult and was viewed as harmful to health. Urban darkness, meanwhile, amplified concerns about moral decay, debauchery, and crime. Much like today, this situation was fuelled by sensationalist reporting by the media, which provoked strong emotional responses in its readers. By contrast, illumination in public space after dark allowed for the exposure and inspection of civil conduct, while maintaining the distance and reserve necessary for liberal subjects to make rational judgements about their own conduct and that of others. Although these developments were not shared globally, their influence spread quickly to many different places around the world, not least due to the ongoing practices of colonisation. Inherent to this process were typically violent forms of dispossession and systematic disadvantaging of Indigenous inhabitants that also included the latter's cultural associations and practices with darkness. Urban illumination thus became synonymous with a particular form of civil behaviour, further consolidating attitudes to both light and dark that have since been exported around the world, though not always peacefully or gently.

Artificial illumination can be seen as instrumental to how cities implement law enforcement. Its capability to initially increase surveillance at night by allowing police officers and security personnel to be able to see more extensively into the urban landscape after dark made its installation a priority for those cities that could afford it. Combined with the more recent development of closed-circuit television and other surveillance technologies, artificial lighting not only provided a major deterrent against crime but also became synonymous with safety, further reinforcing long-held beliefs. From Western perspectives, it is easy, if incorrect, to assume that the reign of light across urban landscapes at night represents an accepted creed. Indeed, we seem to struggle when subjected to sudden or even controlled blackouts, as these appear to be disruptions in social time rather than simply technical failures.[86] Yet darkness is multivalent across time and space, mediated by cultural values and practices that the oppressive tendencies of colonisation did not completely extinguish.

DARK MATTER AND WHITE LIGHT

For many centuries, darkness was believed to rise from the ground, forming night air that could be lethal. This may sound bizarre to us, but it was such a powerful and pervasive myth that it endured until the early 1900s. It drew upon a long-held attachment to the 'miasma theory'. The miasma theory is an obsolete medical theory that contended that diseases—such as cholera, chlamydia, or the Black Death—were caused by a miasma (Ancient Greek for 'pollution'), a noxious form of 'bad air', also known as night air. The theory held that epidemics were caused by miasma emanating from rotting organic matter. The theory was advanced by Hippocrates in the fourth century BC and accepted from ancient times in Europe and China. The theory was eventually abandoned by scientists and physicians after 1880, replaced by the germ theory of disease, that specific germs cause specific diseases.

Based on zymotic theory, people believed that vapours—miasmata—rose from the soil and spread diseases. Many people, especially the weak or infirm, avoided breathing night air by going indoors and keeping windows and doors shut. In addition to ideas associated with zymotic theory, there was also a general fear that cold or cool air spreads disease. The fear of the night air gradually disappeared as understanding about disease increased, as well as improvements in home heating and ventilation. Before the late nineteenth century, however, darkness often signalled more than the temporary absence of light. According to popular cosmology, night fell each evening with the descent of noxious vapours from the sky. Kept at bay by daylight, descending mists reportedly contributed, no less than the sun's departure, to the onset of darkness.[87] Men and women appeared more likely, after dusk, to fall sick and even die. Fears of contagion were intensified by the common perception that illnesses worsened at night due to darkness. In truth, symptoms associated with many illnesses almost certainly grew worse at nighttime, much as they do today.

Deaths themselves, we know, are most likely to occur during the early morning hours, often due to circadian rhythms peculiar to such maladies as asthma, acute heart attacks, and strokes brought on by blood clots accentuated, perhaps, by reduced blood flow to the brain, owing to the position of the body while asleep. In general, we become most vulnerable when the body's circadian cycle is at its lowest ebb. Premodern families typically blamed the dangerous properties of the atmosphere for contributing to respiratory tract illnesses. Two of the most common early modern diseases, influenza and pulmonary tuberculosis, worsened after dark or inflicted added stress on the lungs while bodies lay prone. Tragically, many people might have been saved had their chambers been better ventilated at night, especially when occupied by multiple members of a family. The onset of night also brought with it concerns about the moon's influence on human well-being. When the moon was full, women were believed to be at particular risk of becoming 'lunatics'. The moon was also perceived to impregnate the night air with pestilential damps, widely deemed an even greater menace to human health.

In the early nineteenth century, living conditions in industrialised cities such as those in Britain were increasingly unsanitary. The population was growing at a much faster rate than the infrastructure could support. Manchester's population, for example, which was around 89,000 in 1801, had doubled by the 1820s and then doubled again by 1851 to a total of approximately 400,000, leading to overcrowding and a significant increase in waste accumulation. The miasma theory made sense to the sanitary reformers of the mid-nineteenth century. The Victorian industrial city was one of dirt, dust, and dankness. The artificial lighting of the factories announced its victory over the long-held light–dark cycle and circadian rhythms that had previously underpinned time and work. By reframing and extending the 'working day' into a non-stop, continually functioning endeavour thanks to shift work, the former relationship between labour and time were profoundly altered. Pivotal to this endless labour was the need for constant energy production to power its machinery. The use of coal was essential to this process. The accompanying environmental and health hazards that resulted would lead to commentators of the period, such as the historian Thomas Carlyle, decrying the conditions and using 'Sooty Manchester', which was 'every whit as wonderful, as fearful, unimaginable, as the oldest Salem or Prophetic City.'[88] Its dark spaces, often appearing gloomy even in the daytime, were accurately perceived as inimical to human health. In the latter half of the nineteenth century, new insights into the role of disease and infections due to scientific discoveries concerning epidemiology meant that the idea of night air being detrimental to people's health quickly evaporated.

Modernism in architecture and urban design is often synonymous with light, clarity, and function. It sought to bring order to the built environment through architecture that deployed crisp geometries, austere planes, and frequently, large spans of glazing by using glass, steel, and reinforced concrete. It is important to note that the latter was typically rendered and painted white. In short, modernism ushered 'white light' into cities—across its gleaming façades and reflective surfaces—providing a sharp brilliance of minimalism. Through this architecture, glimpses of the anticipated bright future of cities could be seen. Yet the arrival of these architectural flares in many cities was generally met by an urban landscape creeping out of industrialisation's shadows. This was not simply an issue of form and utility. It was one of material fact. Following the aftermath of the coal-fired furnaces which powered the industrial revolution, many buildings and streets had been coated with soot.[89] The idea that a new order would automatically prevail in cities was immediately confronted by an incoherent, dirty, and dark urban milieu.

Towards the end of the nineteenth century, more and more intensive and expansive lighting arrangements defined specific zones of light and celebrated the city's skyscrapers, bridges, department stores, and theatres. Known as 'white ways' in the US, these brilliantly lit avenues and streets would produce districts that were dazzling.[90] By contrast, poor and blighted areas initially disappeared into the shadows, rendered invisible by their relative darkness. This demarcation would also work the opposite way in the decades of the late twentieth and early twenty-first century as extensive lighting was applied to particular social housing projects and neighbourhoods as an integrated strategy of surveillance and to discourage anti-social behaviour and crime. As with other elements of urban planning, low to mid socioeconomic-status residential areas faced greater inequalities, and this disproportionately affected different racial and ethnic groups, a problem that continues today.[91]

The faith in technological optimism, even utopianism, became widespread after the Second World War. It gathered further momentum through the military-industrial complex of white heat and cold logic—a fascination with atomic power, computer systems, and jet engines. This ushered in new environments that reflected the values of a modern, consumer-oriented society, for whom convenience was analogous with the gleaming surfaces and contraptions of jet airliners and the space age. Culture became smitten with this new dream of a dynamic and streamlined society, for whom the bright and reflective accoutrements of dwellings and leisure illustrated a life being lived well. The shiny, disposable, gadget-laden aspirations that began to permeate and then quickly spread across societies were emblematic of an optimistic, technologically driven future that would mirror the escapism of the post-war period, and it captured the public's imagination. Here was the slick vision of science fiction's tomorrows being brought into the everyday.[92] It was bright, shiny, and often white. The allure of machines and their aesthetics infiltrated popular consciousness. The world briefly appeared as a choreography of technical wizardry, even if the realities were rather more mundane than the experiences shown on TV sets and cinema screens.[93]

It could not last. The peak oil crisis in 1973 steered even more minds towards thinking about the environment and sustainability. Yet this brief respite did little to stem the tide of unbridled growth throughout the late 1970s, 1980s, and beyond. Conspicuous wealth, the collapse of communism in Eastern Europe, privatisation of public services, all signals seemed to promote capitalism with its bright, light future lying ahead. Across the 1990s and the first two decades of the twenty-first century, the built environment became awash with more and more artificial light. Illuminated billboards and animated displays, signage and streetlamps, decorative lighting arrangements on commercial properties and fully lit unoccupied office blocks brought their luminous, competing clutter to cities. The outdoor environment was increasingly brilliant. This growth in the use of artificial lighting at night was not restricted to external space. Within homes, additional lighting came via television sets and other consumer products with illuminated displays. In the latter decades of the twentieth century, the rise of video games and personal computing spawned gaming consoles, laptops, smartphones, and other portable devices that would keep human faces aglow deep into the night.

What does this mean for us and our cities in the twenty-first century? Light still invokes notions of disclosure, surveillance, and security. Dreadful crimes at night, especially male violence against women, have sometimes led to knee-jerk reactions concerning urban lighting, yet ensuring that everyone feels—and is—safe after dark requires appropriate changes in policy and better policing to prevent such violence rather than simply adding more artificial light. As regards the evidence for whether increasing lighting makes people feel safer, it depends on context, and the debates continue.[94] Darkness, for many people, meanwhile, continues to signify the unknown, the secretive, and the other. Positioning darkness as a positive agent for architecture and urban design brings forth an urgent need to better understand the value of different coexistences of light, shade, and dark to the public. This will enable us to provide a socially equitable and environmentally desirable future that promotes civic life differently from business-as-usual approaches, which are predicated on people as consumers. Where is the place for pleasure and joy in cities at night without the pressure to spend money? It is time for us to embrace the darkness and its agency within contemporary urbanism.

Key to achieving this is the reframing of darkness as a positive agent for design. To design with and through darkness rather than against it means we need to significantly alter how many of us encounter it, especially in urban places, through a variety of positive engagements. Throughout history, various artificial lighting technologies have been deployed to help manage and control what occurs in places after dark. This is particularly true of electric lighting which, due to its reliability and uniformity over previous forms of lighting, has become symbolic of modernity and the conquest of nature.[95] Although earlier types of artificial lighting helped people move around, work, and partake in leisure after sunset, electricity ushered in a completely new era of nighttime activity. With the flick of a switch, darkness is banished and the night is transformed. Across innumerable cities around the world, electric light is available, affordable, and usually dependable. In addition, as we have become further connected through globalisation, so too have ideas about how cities should appear at night, with lighting employed as an important signifier of societal and technological progress. Accompanying this change is something profound—darkness is provisional—and so the cycle of day and night, fundamental to much of life on the planet, is also subject to alteration. Normalised through its ubiquity, its multiple benefits, electric light is so intertwined with modern life that we no longer even consider it remarkable.

We reasonably assume that electric light simply illuminates spaces and things that exist rather than altering them through its deployment. This view seriously underestimates the transformative powers of electric light, which, as a form of building material, has radically reconfigured our perception, behaviour, and organisation of cities themselves. The introduction of new luminous spaces and an array of visual conditions that electric light enabled caused a huge shift in how ordinary people encountered and experienced urban places at night.[96] That they also had the power, both literally and symbolically, to transform their domestic spaces with light at their fingertips meant that the spectacular quickly became enmeshed with the mundane. It was not always this way.

Richard Kelly, one of the pioneers of architectural lighting design, drew on his background in stage lighting to introduce a scenographic perspective for architectural lighting in cities. Challenging the engineering mindset that dominated lighting design in the mid-twentieth century, he introduced three principles: focal glow, ambient luminescence, and play of brilliants.[97] Revisiting these principles from the contemporary position of trying to work with rather than against darkness, the diversity and subtleties of lighting promoted by Kelly can be understood to have been quickly lost as urban centres in particular drove artificial illumination into a competing arena where brightness and power became prized over other lighting characteristics. This shift has not gone unnoticed by lighting professionals, who understand all too clearly that the implicit and explicit connotations of this over-illumination are attempts to banish our fear of darkness.[98]

Night, however, is no mere inconvenience for the pristine illusion of architecture and urban design. It is an essential part of our existence. The negative connotations of the night and its frequent companion of darkness endure. Viewed as the time frame for the bad, mad, and terminally sad, night and the dark conjure powerful reactions. Let us be clear about one thing: I am not suggesting that architecture or cities be plunged into a lightless condition, even if such a state were possible. But it is increasingly evident that the indiscriminate blaze of urban illumination is a problem for human and nonhuman health. It is also a barrier to a better connection with the world. The potentialities and capacities of nocturnal ambiances to provide a wider array of sensations and interactions than are often present in urban landscapes compel us to rediscover and reimagine our relationships with darkness.[99] Architecture and cities can offer a spectrum of coexistences between light and dark. Recent shifts in understandings about darkness suggest an opportunity for designers to shape the nocturnal world anew.[100]

To achieve this requires a major rethink in how we perceive the built environment and darkness. Before that, we need to question what we value and desire. Responsible lighting and careful choreography of darkness in urban places can provide important conditions for creativity, culture, socialising, and health and well-being. Rather than blasting the urban fabric with bright artificial light, curating illumination so that it enhances the qualities of place and supports the collective life within it—human and nonhuman— must form a central tenet of how we design for nocturnal citizenry. We need fresh approaches to change the prevailing mindset and encourage us all to reimagine and reconfigure cities between dusk and dawn.

DARKENING CITIES

Over the years, I have worked with many different organisations, groups, and communities who seek to better understand the future, especially how our future cities might be. Let us take a moment to think about this. What might your city look like in ten, twenty, fifty years? Such a question quickly encourages us to reflect, thinking back (not forward!) to places we have perhaps been to or seen. In the case of the latter, this might include fictional examples as well as ones from the real world. We might begin to think of dizzying architecture, spaceship-like forms of mobility, or perhaps, something very similar to how a nearby city looks right now. If we stay with this idea and think a bit longer about this, then we might arrive at a rather different set of questions regarding this future city. What lifestyles will emerge that are different from today's? How might we move around the future city? Where will we live and work? Issues such as these direct us towards thinking about the everyday life of the city, our relationships and interactions within it, and the aspects of these that might be enabled or prove to be barriers.

But wait. Think carefully for a moment and recall the future city that you imagined just now. Was it a bright, shiny, almost frictionless world in which everything worked smoothly? Did it have a blue sky and green spaces, clean surfaces, and imply a safe and healthy environment? Or was it dark and shadowy, a dirty and intimidating built environment ripe for fearsome encounter? Perhaps you imagined something else? Through this quick example, we can understand how readily darkness is diminished by its long-held contrasting relationship with light. This is if we even think about it at all. As a proxy for many negative aspects of the world, the meaning and role of darkness have been reduced to a series of misunderstandings that result in positive perspectives towards its being troublesome. Yet we need darkness. Without it, human life and that of other species face a rapid downward spiral. The challenge, of course, is finding balance. A big obstacle in this regard is that we are so accustomed to artificial light at night in the built environment that it is integral to our expectations of how functioning cities after dark should be.

If we zoom out of the city and start to think about it as part of a network within the wider context of the world, we may reach a very different and somewhat daunting question: how might future cities respond to global challenges and be sustainable? Despite its impact on the planet, widespread use of artificial illumination, particularly in cities, has generally slipped under the radar when we think about environmental issues. Understanding the extent of the problem is a good place to start. In the US alone, the annual average for outdoor lighting energy use is about 120 terawatt-hours, mainly to illuminate streets and parking lots. To give a sense of scale to this, it is enough energy to supply New York City's total electricity needs for two years. DarkSky estimates that at least 30 per cent of all outdoor lighting in the US alone is wasted, mostly by lights that are not shielded.[101] This adds up to $3.3 billion and the release of 21 million tons of carbon dioxide per year. We would have to plant 875 million trees each year to offset all that carbon dioxide.

Tackling light pollution is a significant way to unlock many other urban issues in relation to energy resources, biodiversity, health, and well-being. That these are essential to how we might survive and thrive in the future reinforces the importance of rethinking the coexistences of light and dark in cities. Ensuring ethical, convivial, and sustainable places for everyone and everything should always be a primary concern, but for too long, darkness has been left out of the picture of urban life. In the past, night revolutionised the social landscape. If the onset of darkness resulted in more members of higher authority and status, it also made multitudes of the weak and oppressed more powerful. Freed from the hours of labour and debasement, swathes of people in Europe and America discovered a new sense of purpose at nightfall. The broad appeal of night resonated with the lower orders, being as they were suddenly away from their work and out of the purview of social scrutiny. After sunset, relationships were by choice and typically reflected the close connections of family and friends. Darkness brought with it a physical and psychological shift to the world as symbols and edifices of authority became concealed in the night. This liberation was widespread and provided fertile opportunity for those who had seditious impulses that could not be revealed in the daytime.[102] Nocturnal urbanism, in its early incarnations, was the realm of religious and political minorities, the diseased and the disabled, and homosexuals—essentially all those who were forced to hide their identities during daylit hours or be subject to scorn or punishment. All these groups combined, however, still only accounted for a small proportion of those for whom the cover of night empowered an alternative existence.

The urban night has a long association with freedom, pleasure, and transgression. The expectation of pleasure after dark is a counterpoint to daytime activities generally understood as relating to everyday worlds of work, education, and care. We also know, however, that everyday activities such as convenience shopping or going to the gym have gradually expanded into the early morning or late into the evening, even around the clock. Notions of work and workplace have changed, even more so post-pandemic. It is important to acknowledge that the night is also an assemblage of uneven economic, political, and social geographies as it belies a working population.[103] Many of those who work at night do so due to the limited opportunities they are able to access. This may be reflective of their ethnicity, gender, immigration status, or race, as determined by their context. There have also been important shifts in relation to accessibility and safety for a wider spectrum of different ages, genders, races, and sexual orientations through various movements and organisations.[104] This has generally led to a more inclusive and tolerant attitude towards different communities and groups in some places. In particular, the transition from widely demonised and prohibited activities, which would often seek the cover of darkness for covert and codified behaviours, to more equal rights and less discrimination is positive yet variable. This reminds us that what happens after dark and where is related to wider societal framings, values, and associations. Nocturnal urban places are neither uniform nor alike but consist of social struggles.[105] Moving to a situation where we can promote different levels of darkness in cities will bring about new contests yet are vital for our transition to reducing the impacts of light pollution.

There is no doubt our nights are getting brighter.[106] The extent of this growth has been seriously underestimated. Although LEDs offer a more efficient means of producing artificial light than sodium lamps, the cost benefits have not been accompanied by a reduction in light levels. Quite the opposite. In fact, their implementation has often led to an increase in brightness and energy use. It seems that the concept of light pollution is limited if it is not enabling the necessary changes to lighting design and policy. One way to achieve these is to form new narratives about urban darkness and dark skies to illustrate why the nocturnal world is so important to the well-being of people, planet, and its other inhabitants. Environmental values are essential to this and include us as part of a holistic guiding principle that views humans and nonhumans as integral to the environment, not separate from it.[107] This requires a different philosophical approach to how we relate to darkness in a wider sense before reimagining the role of lighting in cities. We have already discussed the negative connotations that darkness has. Moving from these to a position where darkness is nourishing, restorative, peaceful, and of considerable environmental value is a significant step. In this conception, we are very much part of the environment, and light pollution is a distinctly manufactured problem. This might seem obvious, yet the delamination of ourselves from the wider world is a fundamental issue as we become removed from matters that affect us.

The business-as-usual approach to urban illumination does not question how and why we deploy artificial lighting after dark. This requires fresh perspectives on urban nights, what they are, when, and for whom. There are emerging approaches to the design of nightscapes in cities that actively seek to reconfigure the interplay between artificial light and natural darkness.[108] In France, for example, numerous towns and cities turn off their streetlights to save energy and reduce the impact of light pollution on biodiversity. This action builds upon the country's national light pollution policy, which came into effect at the beginning of 2019 to control the emission of light on outdoor spaces.[109] This new law superseded and repealed the previous one, introduced in 2013, that made it obligatory for businesses, stores, and public buildings in France to turn off lights in shop windows and on façades between 1 a.m. and 6 a.m. Even Paris, also known as the City of Light, as of 2022 has dimmed some of its monuments in response to the energy crisis and President Emmanuel Macron's plea for energy sobriety. It is fair to say that reactions have been mixed. We have become so used to the levels of artificial light at night in urban environments that it can seem shocking and unsettling when they appear darker, even if there is enough light for us to move about.

Many people are familiar with the idea of greening cities, which involves developing and enhancing urban green spaces. By doing so, projects can contribute to preventing loss of biodiversity, reduce air pollution and the impact of heatwaves, achieve climate objectives, and improve the health and well-being of citizens. Please re-read that last sentence. Now, if we were to also start talking about darkening cities in a similar way, we would be able to reach many of these goals in relation to biodiversity, health and well-being of humans and nonhumans, and climate objectives. Clearly, responsible use of lighting technologies comes with an ethical and aesthetic argument for how we want cities after dark to become. Now that we have too much light, it seems logical we can easily resolve this with better designed and implemented lighting. But urban illumination has provided an instrumental role in shaping cities at night, especially how we perceive and encounter darkness, such that we are forced to deal with a conundrum. Any contemporary desire for greater darkness in urban places requires a re-evaluation of urban lighting, which is challenging because it has become enmeshed within the built environment through successive developments and infrastructures.[110] It is also worth noting the flipside of this situation. Although light levels and the amount of light pollution are both increasing, the loss of night is not absolute—that is, not gone forever—but our direct experience with dark skies in cities is usually obstructed or limited by the profusion of street lighting. The comprehensive installation of new lighting, such as LEDs, across a city, as with many strategies to produce uniform and total environments, is unlikely to establish a coherent landscape. This is because the planned power of completeness is an illusion. Apart from those instances of entirely new cities, lighting technology in urban environments is built upon, and responds to, a longer history of partial infrastructures and local characteristics that shape its effects. Therefore, differences persist across the city in ways that are unintended and unforeseen.

We already speak of green and blue elements in our cities, spaces and infrastructures that can enhance biodiversity, mitigate climate change, and improve human health and well-being. If we consider dark skies as a kind of natural infrastructure, with comparable benefits, then we can understand how reimaging urban nature as one of daytime and nocturnal rhythms is a gateway to an entirely new conception of nightlife in cities.[111] Restoring dark skies in cities would enable a more cohesive relationship between built environments and natural ones rather than the sharp distinctions that currently influence our thoughts and actions. Earlier, we spent a few moments thinking about a future city. Darkening cities presents a unique, radical yet viable way to reimagine urban futures and create visions for places that are convivial, ethical, and sustainable.

The endarkened cities of the *Villes Éteintes (Darkened Cities)* (2012) series by photographer Thierry Cohen appear to form a vision of global cities without electricity.[112] Through the collage of a photograph of each of these cities, with an accompanying image taken at a less populated location at the same latitude with greater atmospheric clarity, the compositions offer an alternative view of familiar locations that is striking, poetic, and, perhaps, unsettling. A key aspect of these images is the starry sky that sits above the darkened city in each location. This recurrent theme across the series is a powerful reminder of our connection to the cosmos and the variations of natural darkness, relationships that are currently lost to many urban populations due to light pollution. These images also serve to emphasise the artificiality of cities, highlighting their precariousness and emphasising the wider planetary context and impacts upon its ecologies that urbanisation represents. The series is suggestive of a dramatic future for cities where we are plunged into darkness amidst urban environments that appear to be no longer functional. Such a future may be undesirable, simply a step too far with their spectacular dark skies but no urban illumination. It is a provocative statement with an extreme take on environmental and technological ideas. Our appetite for the type of future hinted at by Cohen is likely to be negligible. The point here is to aim not for cities that are completely dark, but rather, for cities that are darker than they presently are. Precisely how much light should be reduced will vary and be borne by specific contexts and the socio-technical dimensions that inform them. Yet a move towards more responsible and diverse ways of illuminating urban places after dark is urgent and critical. Works such as this project by Cohen encourage us to look beyond the reductive, binary view of light and dark concerning a redistribution of urban darkness.

Dealing with light pollution is sometimes described as being as easy as flicking a switch. If we turned the lights off, then *voilà*, there is darkness! Except this is probably not what we want to achieve. Stringent lights-out measures when implemented in cities have been met with mixed reactions. Plus, as an urbanist, I too want our cities to be vibrant and have collective effervescence at night. The implication is not for cities to try to attain natural darkness in urban centres with no artificial light. Instead, it is about exploring practical pathways to make our cities more resilient, restorative, and beneficial for everyone and everything. The issue, therefore, is where and when we have illumination, how and why it should be responsibly deployed and controlled. This reminds us that light pollution, like darkness, can also be subject to moral arguments. Dark skies are still accessible, but to experience them in cities, we need a holistic strategy that utilises lower levels of lighting, dimming and motion sensors, shielding of lamps and robust regulations to restrict certain forms of light. DarkSky's five principles for responsible outdoor lighting are a good start.[113] The coexistence of light and dark mediates our relationship with place, yet rather than a more-plus-more approach to urban illumination, a greater range of interplay could be implemented. This would re-attune us to the specific characteristics of a city and support nonhuman needs by realigning urban environments with the rhythms of nature. Darkened cities as depicted by Thierry Cohen are not the goal. Moving towards darker cities is the key, and recognising that darkness is relational, partial, and plural is essential. Reimagining and redesigning the city after dark will enable us to embrace alternative conceptions for urban nights.[114] This goes far beyond simply reducing the impact of artificial illumination and involves the flourishing of biodiversity, nocturnal wildlife, and reinstating natural rhythms to support the health of living beings. Recognising the polyphony of nonhuman voices present in nocturnal urban environments, many of which are underrepresented or drowned out by human perspectives, is vital.[115] Novel methods that can account for such thick descriptions are beginning to emerge, yet there remains much more work to be done in support of a multispecies nocturnal urbanism.[116]

The last few years have given significant attention to the potential disruptions and benefits of artificial intelligence. Going back a couple of decades or so, there has also been considerable emphasis placed on the idea of smart cities. The rapid adoption of LEDs as part of an integrated smart system of sensors, artificial intelligence, and appropriate lighting arrangements is an ideal way through which we can explore radical alternatives to how cities after dark can be. Other forms of lighting such as bioluminescence may alter or even replace streetlamps as we currently know them.[117] This will lead to choices. New options about how our future cities might be at night. Cities at night are ideal laboratories for experimentation where our relationship with light and dark is concerned. We can be immersed in all manners of atmospheres and encounter a wide range of multisensory effects, including those borne by the interplay of light and dark.[118] Our experiences of cities at night powerfully shape our perceptions of gloom and, in many ways, reduce our capacity to apprehend the diversity of elements, materialities, and sensations that darkness enriches. An opportunity such as this will quickly disappear if we are not prepared for it, and this requires a profound re-enchantment with darkness, how we think about it, what its significance is, and where and when we want it to be present. This is a multidisciplinary and interdisciplinary challenge that will require collaboration and coordination between the design professions, urban decision- and policy-makers, city leaders, governments, and the public. It is no small task. But it is a timely one.

CLOAK

Midnight. Day is the rehearsal. Night is the performance. As the sun sets, the city of darkness exhales. The air thickens and the dance between dark and light alters its body language. Under the soft gauze of the few remaining sodium oranges, the city's skin softly stirs with anticipation for the night. Its hues and tones merge as the last strokes of daylight withdraw their fingertips from the urban landscape. Now those tiny glimmers, previously imperceptible in the day, become glorious as the shadows stretch and deepen. Here it comes. Slowly, stealthily, stretching out its crepuscular limbs; darkness quietly gathers up the remains of the day in its pockets. They will be handed back over as the cloak of night slips away with the oncoming dawn. But not yet. Before then, the bruised sky and shadows drape across the streets and architecture to transform the familiar into the uncanny and unknown. Exhilaration, liberation, desire, and fear all biding their time in the nocturnal city.

Buildings and streets that seemed familiar now have a different expression. In the meantime, light throws its histrionics around the urban night. Angular and luminous, bright and white, its shapes cut across the city, creating bright planes and overlapping forms, leaving gloomy formations in their wake. This dialogue is held until the glaring headlight beams of a passing vehicle interrupt the conversation and then, moments later, it is reconstructed as the taillights fade. Artificial stars nestle high, blinking red warnings of the towering blocks below. In between these scarlet clusters and the street, nocturnal urban life ebbs and flows. Many people are at rest, settled in their homes and slumber. Others, however, are deliberately out of sync with this pattern as they actively inhabit the urban night. For these people, the nocturnal city is a place and time ripe with potential. They remake the city each night, and in turn, it remakes them.

Tonight, the city is glazed with the frosted kisses of temperatures just below zero. The night air is cold and dense with moisture. Plumes of my breath billow out, brief ghosts of life that dissolve into the surroundings. The freezing air soon holds my face still and silent. Pavements and streets sheen with the gossamer film of ice stretched out in every direction. My feet move tentatively across this urban tundra, finding purchase on their glistening surfaces. Behind me, the slow scrape of a car crackles along the road as salt and ice crunch under its wheels. Above, the architecture folds along the skyline, the boundary between the city and the night sky an ongoing struggle. It is cold tonight. Where possible, people move quickly and quietly through the city. But the slippery coating of the frozen night means that most of the city is drawn into a tender ballet as people and vehicles move cautiously around. Other figures are pressed firmly into doorways and other recesses, the pouches of the city holding them in shadow. The babble of a mobile phone splatters in front of me as a semi-lit face leans into the doorway and listens before firing back a volley of patois. Off-peak dreams and second-hand schemes are being made, out of view of the sleeping city. An electric scooter zips along the brow of the avenue ahead, its whizz-whirr disappearing as fast as it arrived. This is Cheetham Hill on a mid-December night. The clear sky deepens its inky bruise around the city.

The metallic shunt of a roller shutter around the corner breaks the quiet. Moving along Empire Street, I pass silent wholesalers and light industrial units. Pivoting a corner, Sherborne Street takes me into suburbia. Festive lights twinkle and throb along the façades of houses and from within domestic interiors. Starched phantoms of frozen clothing hang rigid along an occasional washing line. The air is damp and dense. There is a palpable emptiness. Few people are about, and little is happening. The soundtrack of the night is muffled—the *gurgle of television sets and music of lives behind bricks and mortar. The fluttering colours of screens run their auroras along the edges of curtains and blinds. The low-rise housing schemes in this area seem to hunker down from the bitter weather. The surrounding landscape is at a more human scale than that of the earlier warehouses or industrial units. But the glacial weather means my feet keep their pace across the night, my body keen to stay warm and on the go. Where other people are briefly glimpsed, they are inanimate, reined in by the cold, with only the blueish white glow of a mobile phone against cheek and hushed tones to indicate life.*

Threading through the warp and weft of suburban streets, Bignor Street Park stretches out ahead of me. A blank, crisp baize awaiting the morning diorama. Onwards and upwards, I am reunited with Cheetham Hill Road just as its curved brow cascades down to Bury Old Road. Along here, the unfurling smells of fried chicken and other takeaway foods whisper of comfort and warmth against the night. Swirls of steam escape doors and windows as deep fat fryers plunge and sizzle behind glass windows and acrylic counters. Delivery drivers wait inside doorways, embracing the brief respite from the cold, ready to transport the tasty food in their insulated cubes to hungry nocturnal neighbourhoods. Above their heads, a psychedelic frieze of illuminated signs follows me along the road, a kaleidoscope of colours, fonts, and anthropomorphic characters. An idling taxi puffs its fumes and thrums with the low bass of its sound system, on top of which is the animated shrill of a driver voicing his half of a conversation into a phone. His untethered hands add flourishes to the speech as if conducting the scene beyond his windscreen.

Three teenagers, hoodied and huddled, a six-legged life form scoping out its surroundings and chittering its way along the pavement in fast slang and furtive glances. Their intense sound bubble floats by and out of earshot. In its wake, the retail landscape consolidates, boxes of brick and glass with nearby car parking for customer convenience. Not now though. At this late hour the place is deserted and the surfaces gleam with a layer of frost. The friendly choreography of cooks, customers, and couriers is on display in different formations along a string of takeaway restaurants. Heat, grease, and strong aromas waft through the air, leaking out of doorways and opened polystyrene boxes. Pizzas and kebabs, chicken and chips, curry and rice, and other hot treats to nourish those who share the night. Aside from the street theatre adjacent to the takeaways, the rest of the street is silent with its shuttered shopfronts.

Turning back on myself, I return uphill and then down along a curve of townhouses and back into a suburb, this time Crumpsall. Many of the homes along this stretch are semi-detached, conjoined architecture keeping two families apart by a membrane of wallpaper, plaster, and brick. Lives are largely muffled, noise kept firmly within domestic spaces save for the occasional one-sided chatter from a passing mobile phone user or the sporadic speech that slips through the night's cracks and crevices. Sound and place become weirdly dissonant. The general quiet envelops the area, akin to a vast blanket, yet because of the cold air and the absence of sound, when a noise does appear, its presence somehow strikes a pertinent chord by contrast. This soundscape is one of deteriorating loops, circadian rhythms of family life slowly and steadily disintegrating in pitch and timbre as the darkness grows in the night. From navy blue sky and ochre clouds to a more solidified bruise of purple blacks. Feeling uncanny and out of sync with this muted orchestra, I stop. Breathe in. Breathe out. Breathe in. Breathe out. Breathe in. Breathe out.

I walk into Crumpsall Park, dark velvet-frost lawns flank each step, with the spongy shadow forms of trees that stand in attendance to line the paths and perimeter. There is no one else here tonight, as the obelisk, empty play area, and tennis courts can attest. Gathering momentum, I stride back out of the park and into the streets again. I am an instrument in this cold world, alert to the noises I make. My boots pad along the pavement in dull clomps, suddenly replaced by the scritch-scratch of gravel beneath my feet, then back to the subdued percussion again. I re-tune, watching the trams glide away on their curvatures into the infinity of night. I follow the slope down the arterial road. Synagogues are gathered, and then there is a pause before mosques present themselves in the streetscape and skyline. The derelict St Luke's

Church stands solemnly inside its unlit graveyard. No bicycle couriers seeking sanctuary in there tonight.

From this point, the road rolls its asphalt down to the city centre. Large retail parks shoulder into view, their stripped-down sheds offering discounted desires and free parking. Behind this budget landscape, North Street peels away from the main thoroughfare, and with it, a longer history of light industrial units slowly unfurls. This is a micro-utopia of demand and supply. Few things or services cannot be bought around here, as it provides the city with portals to the world through its procurement and logistics of goods and services. Electric light weakly blooms within fogged windows or along the cold steel of a door, yet whatever operations are happening, they remain clandestine. The ghosts of intense and poorly paid labour hang heavy around here. A formerly white plastic seat, since speckled with the patina of grit and grime, waits to receive a tired body and provide brief respite from work. Little gatherings of cigarette butts close to façade apertures rest quietly, following a flick and then the arc of their flight from fingers. They are tiny reminders of the soundscape from the day before, spectres of routine and all-too-temporary recuperation. The sleeping hulk of an HGV lies hard against the kerb, its smell of rubber and grit telling tales of highways and byways near and far. Its wide eyes and festive cabin lights sit forlorn and discharged from power. The confetti of foam packing material twitch in the breeze, but the long ribbons of sponge nearby are unwilling to join the dance tonight. The jabber of the unseen city beckons, its babble ebbing and flowing around corners and along streets in relation to my navigation across the patchwork of the urban fabric. Arcing back again towards the main thoroughfare of Cheetham Hill Road, along which cars and trucks shift to and from the urban centre, their bright white headlights growing, their blood-red rear lights dissipating into the long avenue. Hydraulics squeak, stereos pump beats, while further away some light rail transport adds metallic streaks of noise.

Turning back into the city centre, it is striking how being hidden in plain sight Cheetham Hill is both a promise and a premise. It offers countless opportunities for reinvention in its environs and the ability to have encounter and exchange with a diverse and mobile set of cultures and identities. Its steadfast refusal to acquiesce to the planned power of the city and the latter's ongoing quest for an urban renaissance of renewal have led to its character as much as the forces of late capitalism have shaped its offer of cheap and counterfeit goods, shady operations, and both legitimate and illicit provisions to the wider population. With the return of LED-illuminated hues in the sky, the very radiance of the city centre, it is time to leave the early hours of the urban landscape behind for another night.

DARK FUTURES

HOW BRIGHT SHOULD OUR FUTURE BE?

The field of future studies is the systematic, interdisciplinary, and holistic study of advancement, often with the aim of exploring how people will live and work in the future. Although it can encompass a diversity of subjects and trends, including environmental and social dimensions of life, a significant proportion of future studies work is undertaken following the potential impact of technology. Known also as *futures research*, *futurism*, or *futurology*, the field of future studies seeks to understand what is probable in terms of continuing and what might plausibly change. More recently, the idea of preferable futures has raised related questions about who the future is for and in whose preference is it shaped, and how and why. Predictive techniques, such as forecasting, can be applied, but the contemporary future studies field has widened to encourage the exploration of alternative futures and deepened to examine the worldviews and mythologies that underlie our collective prospects. The discipline seeks a systematic and pattern-based understanding of past and present and to explore the possibility of future events and trends. By contrast to the physical sciences, where a specific system is examined, future studies work concerns a much larger and more complex world system. Future studies work can attract scepticism yet is increasingly adopted by governments, corporations, NGOs, etc. as they try to make sense of what happens in the long term and its potential impacts.

In a world that now seems more uncertain and volatile than ever before due to the impacts of human activity, future studies work is being used to help leaders and communities navigate their way through complex potential scenarios and increase their resilience. Future studies have the capacity to be diverse, imaginative, analytically insightful, ethically engaged, and practically applied. However, a considerable number of people have limited ability to envision alternative futures. How might things be different? The core challenge that this work addresses is often global, but it can also be understood as psychological. It is a fundamental aspect of the human condition that we long to know what will happen next, across a range of scales, from the personal to the planetary. The challenge, then, is how to engage the various possible worlds we might find ourselves in later, not just as an intellectual exercise, abstract and removed from us, but also more deeply as potential lived realities. It is here that I think 'dark futures' can make an important contribution to our daily (or perhaps nightly might be better) routines and other ways of being in the world.

To date, future studies has been strong in producing frameworks for organising thinking, but far less so in terms of translating these anticipations into embodied insights. This raises an important question: Is thinking about the future a privilege or a right?[119] With many people facing hardship, pressures of everyday existence, notwithstanding abject poverty, the impacts of extreme weather, climate change, and war, spending time engaged with the longer term may be literally unthinkable. People are generally unfamiliar with thinking about futures and tend to dismiss them. And yet, as human beings, irrespective of our physical limitations, we enjoy—and well we should—a capacity to wander freely in the imagination. To hope, to dream, to create alternatives is central to us and the ways we are in the world. The most useful tradition of future studies is one notable for being radically imaginative, critical, inclusive, and democratic. This requires the 'future' to be reclaimed from progressive ideologies that historically led to the different ways in which it has been abused, colonised, or pre-populated with a huge amount of baggage.

The future is not something that simply happens to us but something we can shape. If we reflect on how darkness has usually been thought about and discredited, we can sense the potential to alter this thinking by reframing and reconfiguring its role in our lives. Yet how futures are portrayed simply reinforces the binary opposition between light and dark. Through its long-held associations with the good, clarity, and wisdom, light is imbued in evocative descriptions of futures with notions of cleanliness, shimmering, and trouble-free worlds that are usually alloyed to significant technological advancement. Darkness, meanwhile, is deployed in descriptions of futures that are necessarily problematic by inference. Whether by using shadows to cover unseen things or by coatings of grime and dirt that obscure the world or a blackened landscape and/or sky that suggests ecological collapse, the dark is a signifier of something difficult and often bad.

In Isaac Asimov's short story 'Nightfall', the planet Lagash is in a state of perpetual illumination due to the six suns of its star system.[120] Although there are areas of darkness inside caves and tunnels, etc., 'night' does not exist. Scientists claim to have discovered evidence of numerous ancient civilisations on Lagash, all destroyed by fire about every 2000 years apart. With another collapse seemingly imminent, according to their predictions, due to an eclipse that will obscure one of the suns when it is alone in the sky, the narrative unfolds. The planet's inhabitants have an instinctive and intense fear of the dark, having evolved with no diurnal cycle. The scientists theorise that earlier civilisations were destroyed by people who went insane during previous eclipses as they started large fires, due to their desperation for light, which quickly went out of control. However, what the scientists have not anticipated is the appearance of stars when Lagash is plunged into darkness. When it emerges, the night sky is filled with the dazzling light of more than 30,000 stars, the first that people on the planet had ever seen. Upon learning of their apparent insignificance within a vast universe, coupled with the global darkness of the eclipse, everyone loses their sanity. The light of spreading flames moving across the landscape shifts from a glowing entity in the distance to an engulfing force that subsumes society.

This unquenchable thirst for light and inability to deal with darkness is not a bad allegory for our times. I doubt that the global human population would be driven to an existential climax upon all being able to see the stars in the night sky. But, due to our disconnection with dark skies, we are endangering ourselves and countless other nonhuman lives. It could be argued that this is precisely what we have been busy doing for centuries, a process which has rapidly accelerated throughout the twentieth century and early decades of the twenty-first century: banishing darkness in favour of light, irrespective of the consequences. The impact of this effects everything. It is environmental, social, political, technological, economic, and global in its reach. As our planet rotates in the darkness of the universe, our avarice has overtaken us. Through the extraction of resources, the pollution of land, air, and oceans, and the vanquishing of darkness, we have all but delaminated ourselves from the world. By doing so, we have hypnotised ourselves with an illusion—the mastery of time and space. Yet this is not so.

The wider world, whilst reeling from the impacts of human activity, care little about our small plans and relentless quest to conquer new domains. Most recently, it is our attention that has been held hostage—our eyes are now the prize—for the endless scrolling of clickbait, advertisements, fake news, misinformation, and the kernels of truth that can quickly become co-opted and defamed. Under this permanent glare, our lives are whitewashed as differences and nuances become coated with the sheen of light. Dark corners, meanwhile, are further relegated to the dispossessed, the disenfranchised, the disillusioned, and the deviant, as far as mainstream society is concerned. This is a big mistake.

Assuming we could look upon the stars at night, we would be reminded of the remarkable yet precarious position we find ourselves in here on Earth.[121] It is not too late. Our collective future depends on collaboration, coordination, and cooperation. This is no mean feat and will require immense creativity and imagination. This is where dark futures play their crucial role in what happens next. If, as I hope this book has illustrated, we can understand the benefits of going beyond our present and long-held problems with darkness to imagine a coexistence that is resilient and sustainable, inclusive and equitable, human and more-than-human, local and global, then our futures can be healthy and vibrant. Our ability to reshape the planet has been demonstrated before. It is now time to put this capability into better guiding principles and practices that will mitigate some of the worst effects of climate change, enable future generations to flourish, and share our planet gracefully with those who cannot speak for it.

It was not so long ago that the impacts humans had were limited to our planet. On 4 October 1957, all this would change. That was the launch date of *Sputnik*, the first manufactured satellite sent into space by the Soviet Union to orbit Earth. Another pivotal moment occurred on 7 December 1972, when a photograph was taken by the crew of the *Apollo 17* spacecraft on its way to the Moon. Officially designated as photograph AS17-148-22727 by NASA, the image was cropped and chromatically adjusted. It became known as *The Blue Marble* due to the astronauts' description of what they saw when looking back at Earth. Although it was not the first clear colour photograph to be taken of an illuminated face of the planet, images had been produced by satellites since 1967, it is significant since it was the first time such an image with the whole planet visible was taken by a person. In the original image, the darkness of space takes up about three-quarters of the photograph.[122] The manipulated image, which is far more commonly found, centres on Earth as if we are the most important thing amidst all the celestial majesty. It is, of course, somewhat inevitable that we would focus on our home within the seemingly limitlessness of space. It also belies the subsequent mess we leave beyond the atmosphere of our planet in our treating space as the new frontier with the attempts at colonisation and accompanying space junk that results.

Almost exactly forty years later, on 5 December 2012, NASA released a nighttime view of Earth called *Black Marble* which illustrated all the anthropogenic and natural phenomena that glows detectably from space.[123] Composite satellite imagery was then produced by using filtering techniques to observe dim signals including city lights, gas flares, auroras, wildfires, and reflected moonlight. To emphasise the urban illumination at night, all the auroras, fires, and other forms of natural light were removed. As beguiling as such imagery is, it presents a double-edged premise. On the one hand, it provides a valuable tool for research on light pollution, disaster impacts, human settlements, and energy infrastructures, etc. Yet, on the other hand, it continues a problematic narrative about the relationship between light and dark, including what should be shown and omitted.[124] For the picture we see is a composite image subject to considerable manipulation, not least where darkness resides and where it does not. It is far from neutral and brings us back, almost full circle, to where we began at the start of this book, beset with commonly held perceptions of light as good and darkness as bad. That these binary oppositions, as shown throughout this book, have been strongly reinforced throughout history in different ways and, for various reasons, is reflective of their cultural conditions and context. However, these have become unmoored and washed adrift, polluting other fathoms of thought in their wake. Such leaky vessels have been mistaken for safe harbours. Unquestioning acceptance of outdated arguments and moral imperatives that have typically subjugated the poor, the female, and non-white men have led to the current state of affairs.

What does this mean for futures? Why should they so often be presented as a shimmering oasis, and what does this say about the elements that are left out? Despite the overall plea of this book, regarding the remarkable qualities and capacities that darkness presents, we should not overlook the aspect of how ordinary it can be. Perhaps it is because we think of darkness as something always there, providing the backdrop to our nightly rhythms and routines, that it has been taken for granted. We have also not noticed its gradual disappearance as more and more artificial light at night has entered our lives. How might futures be envisioned if we accepted their ordinariness? Rather than the shiny, glitch-free worlds of tomorrow, where is the debris, dust, and darkness to be found? This has all to do with being grounded. Such futures may not necessarily be mundane, yet they help remind us that things will need cleaning, fixing, or replacing. If we follow this line of thought, we can question existing conventions in the world and query what might happen if we lived differently. Key to this is the everyday and, crucially, everynight experiences that our lives imprint upon our environment and those we share it with.

The practicalities of living on a damaged planet that requires urgent restoration are not evident in the projections made for technologically driven futures such as smart cities. In these visions, urban environments are presented as gleaming, shimmering miniature worlds of transparent surfaces and greenery. Although visually enticing, many such urban futures conceal the accretive nature of how cities evolve and remove the challenges and obstacles of clean energy production, let alone the issues of maintaining them free of detritus. This drive towards a perfectly choreographed world for urban life, in which interactions and sequencing are akin to the elaborate stage set of *The Truman Show* (1998) is of course practically impossible even if it were desirable.

Places at night are powerful evocations of a future that is partially present and in the process of becoming. This is because there are enough features to define a place, but it also feels unfinished and open to reinterpretation. Nocturnal cities are capable of being both weird and eerie. Darkness is alive with potentialities. It stirs creativity and the imagination. It offers us a realm within and through which we can explore alternatives, the other side of the mirror, if you will. At night the streets become supernatural, even magical. Not in the literal sense that they are full of ghosts. Rather, in a way that the past feels more palpable at night; it seems to leak out of the city's pores amidst the shadows. This otherworldliness is essential if we are to have the time and place to reimagine the world and how we might collectively live in it in the future. Accepting that the future is not written is important. Also, recognising that the midwifing of futures might occur in what is overlooked, neglected, or marginal is vital. It is within the shadowlands of the imagination and our world where we will best find alternatives to the business-as-usual pathways that have led us this far into the light.

To 'go dark' is to stop all communication or activities, usually temporarily but often for a significant period, if not indefinitely. If we reclaim this term in a positive way, what might this mean for us? Rather than a form of ghosting, corporate sneaking, or military strategy, we could and should embrace going dark as a vital part of redressing the chaos of always being on, always connected. Down, down in the darkness there is calm. A necessary restorative time and place for rest and recuperation. While there has been much-needed emphasis on the negative impacts of light pollution on nocturnal creatures, we must not underestimate how ruinous disrupting the circadian rhythms of any living beings is.[125] It is quite simply unnatural. And disastrous. A form of ecocide that we have created and continue to perpetuate to the detriment of ourselves, other forms of life, and the precious planet we share.

Understanding the spectrum of darkness, its diversity, and nuances is crucial to our collective life going forward and for the generations that will follow. Darkness intersects the ecological, cultural, astronomical, and bio-physiological spans across time and space. To attend to rather than recoil from darkness will play a fundamental role in the recovery of our planet, enabling biodiversity to flourish and benefiting human health. At a practical level, the loss of access to darkness, associated with the negative impacts of excessive illumination, is not a problem of knowledge. It is not a problem of technological capacity. Nor is it necessarily a problem of political will. It does, however, reflect our inertia. Slowly but surely, unchecked excessive artificial illumination at night is altering our world, ourselves, and countless other nonhuman lives. Thinking and working with dark futures is, therefore, a valuable way to counter this trend.

DARK FUTURES NOW
AND NEXT

For as long as humans have been around, we have longed to know what lies ahead.[126] For thousands of years, we have sought to control, manage, predict, and understand the future. The use of astrology to read the stars, philosophical debates, creative visions, or scientific analysis of data for patterns and trends, all are ways in which we have attempted to know what the future might bring. The ubiquity of the word 'future' in our lives and wider society reflects the accelerated rate of change that we face. Whereas previous eras had apparent certainties, such as ecological stability, the Anthropocene has meant that these are becoming difficult to discern in a world that is increasingly complex, ambiguous, uncertain, and volatile. How we address the future, therefore, is also becoming harder and harder. Faced with its challenges, we don't have to look far to discover lots of different organisations, communities, and groups actively engaged in trying to better comprehend the future. Driving much of this work is the potential to influence the future, with a focus on technology.[127] Let's not kid ourselves; the future is also the domain of significant business conducted by agencies, consultancies, government bodies, military organisations, and many others. Futurology is abundant with the notion of 'shedding light' on what could happen next as if we can glimpse it within the darkness of the not-yet that lies before us.

A vital part of how we might respond to the complex conditions of futures is education. If we can gain knowledge, understand alternatives and their implications for the future of collective life around the planet, including us, then chances are we are more likely to engage with it. The idea that we are all moving toward a common, singular future has been contested. This notion has been questioned since the mid-twentieth century, when the scientific positivist concept of a single future could be usefully challenged. Many futurists realised that seeking to predict the future in this way was not the most useful for thinking about the complexity of the world. As the field of future studies evolved in the early 1980s, Johan Galtung was an early advocate of different types of futures, referring to *probable futures, possible futures,* and *preferred futures*.[128] Probable futures usually relate to extrapolation of trend data and verge towards more negative forecasts. Possible futures, meanwhile, embrace imagination and creativity in the production of alternative visions. Preferred futures relate to and include critical and normative values. A fourth type, *prospective futures*, identified by Åke Bjerstedt, relates to activism when confronted with probable futures.[129] Of relevance to us here is the overall shift from positivism to pluralism. The former is rooted in the hard sciences and predicates an empiricist approach to 'the future'. The latter originates from the social sciences and promotes a diversity of approaches to 'multiple futures'.

It makes sense to think of dark futures in their multiplicity, since they will be diverse. We know that darkness is not homogeneous, nor are the perceptions of it. Multiple dark futures will coexist, as currently there are multiple presents across different geographies and societal contexts, experienced differently by those in them. It is unrealistic to expect everyone to agree on a singular dark future, nor would this be desirable. As with any substantial shift in human attitudes, behaviours, or values, things get complex.

When we consider dark futures, there is no one-size-fits-all solution that can be seamlessly deployed around the world. Darkness itself is relational, situated, and diverse. Responses will therefore need to evolve carefully from the specific contexts in which they are conceived to ensure acceptance and adoption of practical interventions. This 'staying with the trouble' rather than focusing on neat yet ultimately flawed solutions is essential.[130] Prior to any action will be a profound shift in thinking that enables our dark ideologies to positively influence our technologies for the benefit of the many ecologies around our world.

There is, perhaps inevitably, lots of overlap but also tensions amongst the different aspects of darkness within this book. Ensuring climate and social justice for all is paramount. That includes all those whose voices may not be easily heard or have representation, whether human or nonhuman. Ideas concerning the future emerge and echo over time, while others seem to lie conceptually exhausted in history. That people, having found a way to sustain collective life in the future for humanity and our nonhuman neighbours on Earth, might look back on a book such as this with the benefit of hindsight and wonder what all the fuss was about would be encouraging, but the pathways there seem less obvious at this moment—we are in the dark, but now with a different understanding of it. Entanglements with darkness, whether ideological, ecological, or technological, keep us grounded in the difficulty of the world. What is clear, however, is that the seeds of these futures are likely already sown in the minds of those that will co-create them and those generations that will follow.

To think of the future as something distant from us would be to underestimate our collective agency and responsibility. Visions are created as ways of expressing the things that have not happened yet and perhaps never will, or will but in a different, possibly unanticipated manner. Both the content and format of these articulations shape our ideas of, and intentions towards, futures. This is especially true of dark visions, which emanate positive qualities of gloom for our existence, that of other species, and the environments we share. In an era of rapid transformations and global uncertainties, it would be easy to find solace through clarity and agreement rather than address the complexity of the task ahead of us. It is suggested here that articulating divergence is a crucial step in exploring radical alternatives and being able to fully appraise their respective values and limitations. Dark futures offer a vital alternative to radically reconceptualise how we think about the ways we live and their impacts on the planet across a range of scales: domestic, neighbourhood, city, national, and planetary. Moving away from solution-orientated approaches to understand them as part of a considerably wider range of methods enables us to envision alternatives and gain knowledge of the underlying similarities, tensions, and contradictions. Through this process, we can critically question assumptions about what futures are, who they are for, why they are desirable, and how and when they are to be brought into being. Without a sense of knowing which options are available to us, the limited pathways that dominate our view obscure significant ways forward—we are dazzled by their brightness as they whitewash radical alternatives out of view. This is the significance of dark futures for tomorrow's world and their relevance for our collective life. It is time to change how we think about darkness. We need new stories to help galvanise the action and commitment needed. To embrace dark futures is to make sense of entangled histories, situated narratives, and thick descriptions that can support collective life in all its forms on Earth.[131]

Rather than simply having hope for the dark, we need to bring about the changes needed both individually and collectively to enable darkness to flourish. More than ever, we need balance. Healthy coexistences of light and dark for all our lives and for those that will follow, human and nonhuman. The transitions needed to rebalance our relationship with Earth and the countless other species we share it with are mind-boggling. It is no surprise we prefer to look the other way. In fact, many of us are so accustomed to thinking of and experiencing light in certain ways that we are not aware of what we are missing. For such a shift to occur at the global scale, it will require a form of collaboration, cooperation, and commitment that is possible, yet in the present may not seem plausible. Making this happen will, to some extent, necessitate it to be preferable, that is, we must need and desire this. Pulsing through the tributaries of such positive change must be the vessels that carry forward this enormous task. This flotilla will be subject to considerable challenges—the stormy weather of political, cultural, and economic spheres that influence where we are and the direction in which we are heading. Yet undercurrents that may enable this passage into the mainstream are detectable. The ideological drift of darkness from regressive to positive is already underway. This is critical. We need to acknowledge that our relationship with artificial light has become slavish. The illusion of progress as synonymous with more and more light is twentieth-century thinking. We are already in the third decade of the twenty-first century, and the time to overcome the barriers to thinking in this way are long overdue. Darkness is progressive. It signifies the very act of being alive as a species that depends on circadian rhythms for survival. Our ability to flourish depends entirely on rethinking our values and restoring our interrelationships with the planet and its other inhabitants. For too long we have distanced ourselves from the ways in which the natural world works, in our quest for betterment. That our interactions with the environment and, increasingly, with one another are becoming further mediated is only serving to widen this disconnection. The time to act is now.

Dark skies are vital to this future. They are the nocturnal commons, and access to them is a clear signal that we can do better. They also represent the overlap of the aesthetic, scientific, and spiritual. Much of human knowledge and understanding of Earth and the universe beyond was through being able to connect with the stars in the night sky. Let us not forget that we ourselves are made of stars. Nearly all the elements that make up the human body come from stars. Dark skies are our shared heritage, threading us back across history to our origins and forward to a planet that can be equitable, just, and sustainable for all collective life, of which we are but a part. Instead of something to be fearful of, dark futures represent an essential step-change in our thinking, our values, our actions, and our nature. This is the task set before us; we must trust each other to deliver upon it and tend to its ongoing endeavour for the benefit of all life on Earth.

Although I have focused on darkness as an idea, across this book I have also sought to illustrate how important a shift in thinking is prior to action. At a time when the anthropogenic impacts upon the planet are more devastating than ever, we urgently need to rethink what we are doing, how we are doing it, and why we are doing it. This includes whitewashing in all its forms and its equally insidious sibling, greenwashing. The transfer of certain ideas through globalisation has led to a flattening of culture and the differences of place. In their wake, many urban environments have often become ablaze with unnecessary artificial lighting, while others appear to languish in the shadows of informal or unreliable infrastructures, desperately seeking to be awash with the perceived brilliance of progressive development. Spatial justice and enabling all communities to be able to benefit from the safety and security of dependable access to resources is an important step, one the Sustainable Development Goals of the United Nations rightly strives for. However, as this book has shown, the cost of light goes far beyond any economic definition, disrupting the health and well-being of humans and other species, steering us all towards the collapse of ecosystems.

We can change this situation for the better. It does not have to be this way. We need to form a more holistic, relational, and nuanced knowledge of darkness and develop new ways of working with it rather than against it. Such an endeavour will require us to embrace the irreducibility, multiplicity, and unknowability of the world, especially darkness, to foster our imagination and creativity towards ways that effect beneficial change for collective life, humans and nonhumans, based on principles of uncertainty. This is important and urgent. Darkness in all its forms is under threat. Together, we can flourish alongside the many other forms of life on this planet, rather than at their expense, if we move towards dark futures. It is time for the lights to go down before we extinguish ourselves. This affects everyone and everything.

We dream in darkness.

NOTES

Into darkness

1. David Wallace-Wells, 'Cascades', in *The Uninhabitable Earth: A Story of the Future* (London: Penguin, 2019), pp. 1–36.

2. See, for example, the diversity of contributions in Nick Dunn and Tim Edensor (eds), *Rethinking Darkness: Cultures, Histories, Practices* (London: Routledge, 2020).

3. This is something Paul Cureton and I sought to unpack by proposing Social Futures and Global Futures alongside Technological Futures in Nick Dunn and Paul Cureton, *Futures Cities: A Visual Guide* (London: Bloomsbury, 2020).

4. A. Roger Ekirch, *At Day's Close: A History of Nighttime* (London: Weidenfeld & Nicolson, 2005).

5. For a poetic navigation between her personal perceptions of the dark polar night of northern Norway and meditations on the wider meanings of darkness, see Sigri Sandberg, *An Ode to Darkness*, trans. Siân Mackie (London: Sphere, 2019).

6. John E. Bortle, 'Introducing the Bortle Dark-Sky Scale', in *Sky & Telescope* 101:2 (February 2001), pp. 126–129.

7. Drawing on Zen Buddhism and African and Native American Indigenous traditions, darkness as a cosmic landscape is explored by

Zenju Earthlyn Manuel, *Opening to Darkness* (Boulder, CO: Sounds True, 2023).

8. See, for example, Marion Dowd and Robert Hensey (eds) *Darkness: Archaeological, Historical and Contemporary Perspectives* (Oxford: Oxbow Books, 2016), and Nancy Gonlin and April Nowell (eds) *Archaeology of the Night: Life After Dark in the Ancient World* (Boulder, CO: University Press of Colorado, 2018).

9. Bryan D. Palmer, *Cultures of Darkness: Night Travels in the Histories of Transgression* (New York, NY: Monthly Review Press, 2000).

10. The increase in wakeful activity stretching beyond daylit hours was discussed in the seminal article by Murray Melbin, 'Night as Frontier', in *American Sociological Review* 43:1 (February 1978), pp. 3–22.

11. Regarding the industrialisation of the night and the impact it has had upon people and notions of work, see Jonathan Crary, *24/7: Late Capitalism and the Ends of Sleep* (London: Verso, 2013).

12. Anna Levin, *Incandescent: We Need to Talk About Light* (Salford: Saraband, 2019).

13. Stuart Clarke, *Beneath the Night: How the Stars Have Shaped the History of Humankind* (London: Guardian Faber Publishing, 2020).

14. For example, Elisabeth Bronfen, *Night Passages: Philosophy, Literature, and Film*, trans. Elisabeth Bronfen with David Brenner (New York, NY: Columbia University Press, 2013).

15. The impossibility of trying to quantify the value of the night sky is examined in David Henderson, 'Valuing the Stars: On the Economics of Light Pollution', in *Environmental Philosophy* 7:1 (Spring 2010), pp. 17–26. https://www.jstor.org/stable/26168027

16. For a range of different creative engagements with dark skies alongside insights into their contemporary resonance see Nick Dunn and Tim Edensor (eds), *Dark Skies: Places, Practices, Communities* (London: Routledge, 2023).

17. This term was originally coined by Robert M. Pyle, 'The Extinction of Experience', in *Horticulture* 56 (1978), pp. 64–67. Yet as our detachment from the rest of the living world has increased, this idea has been taken up again more recently, for example, Masashi Soga and Kevin J. Gaston, 'Extinction of Experience: The Loss of Human-Nature

Interactions', in *Frontiers in Ecology and the Environment* 14:2 (March 2016), pp. 94–101.

18. As access to dark skies increasingly disappears, recent nature writing has been keen to celebrate their wonder, for example, Tiffany Francis, *Dark Skies: A Journey into the Wild Night* (London: Bloomsbury, 2019) and Matt Gaw, *Under the Stars: A Journey into Light* (London: Elliott & Thompson, 2020).

19. See Sarah-Jane Downing, *The English Pleasure Garden 1660–1860* (Oxford: Shire Publications Ltd., 2009), p. 22.

20. David E. Nye, *American Illuminations: Urban Lighting, 1800–1920* (Cambridge, MA: The MIT Press, 2018).

21. See, for example, William C. Sharpe, *New York Nocturne: The City After Dark in Literature, Painting and Photography, 1850–1950* (Princeton, NJ: Princeton University Press, 2008).

22. I am reminded of the description of flying into Los Angeles, '[a] sort of luminous, geometric, incandescent immensity, stretching as far as the eye can see, bursting out from the cracks in the clouds', by Jean Baudrillard, *America*, trans. Chris Turner (London: Verso, 1988), p. 51.

23. For example, Catherine Rich and Travis Longcore (eds) *Ecological Consequences of Artificial Night Lighting* (Washington DC: Island Press, 2006).

24. The dependency of our humanity upon the wider more-than-human natural world is examined in David Abrams, *The Spell of the Sensuous: Perception and Language in a More-Than-Human World* (New York, NY: Random House, 1996).

25. Ron Chepesiuk, 'Missing the Dark: Health Effects of Light Pollution', in *Environmental Health Perspectives* 117:1 (January 2009), A20–A27. https://doi.org/10.1289/ehp.117-a20

26. Elizabeth Kolbert, *The Sixth Extinction: An Unnatural History* (London: Bloomsbury, 2014).

Darkling

27. This transition is discussed in more detail in Nick Dunn, 'Dark Futures: The Loss of Night in the Contemporary City?' in *Journal of*

Energy History / Revue d'Histoire de l'Énergie, Special Issue: Light(s) and Darkness(es) / Lumière(s) et Obscurité(s), 1:2 (March 2019), pp. 1–27. http://energyhistory.eu/en/node/108

28. Gustave Doré and Blanchard Jerrold, *London: A Pilgrimage* (London: Grant & Co., 1872).

29. This notion is explored further in my previous book, Nick Dunn, *Dark Matters: A Manifesto for the Nocturnal City* (New York: Zer0 Books, 2016).

30. The relationship between the real and the imaginary, writing and cities after dark is examined in Nick Dunn, 'Nyctopolis: The City of Darkness', in *"Invisible Cities" and the Urban Imagination*, ed. Benjamin Linder (London: Palgrave, 2022), pp. 337–348.

Ideologies

31. Roger T. Ames and David L. Hall, *Dao De Jing: A Philosophical Translation* (New York, NY: Ballantine Books, 2003).

32. For an exposition of how the hierarchical approach of favouring light over darkness traces back to ancient civilisations see Hans Blumenberg, 'Light as Metaphor for Truth: At the Preliminary Stage of Philosophical Concept Formation', in *Modernity and the Hegemony of Vision*, ed. David Michael Levin (Berkeley, CA: University of California Press, [1957] 1993), pp. 30–62.

33. René Descartes, *The Philosophical Writings of Descartes, Vol. II*, trans. John Cottingham, Robert Stoothoff and Dugald Murdoch (Cambridge: Cambridge University Press, 1984).

34. For example, https://www.space.com/dark-energy-what-is-it

35. Here I am indebted to the nuanced analysis and discussion provided by Steven Burik, 'Darkness and Light: Absence and Presence in Heidegger, Derrida, and Daoism', in *Dao: A Journal of Comparative Philosophy* 18 (2019), pp. 347–370. https://doi.org/10.1007/s11712-019-09670-7 Also see respectively, Martin Heidegger, *Bremen and Freiburg Lectures: Insight Into That Which Is and Basic Principles of Thinking*, trans. Andrew J. Mitchell (Bloomington, IN: Indiana University Press, 2012), and Jacques Derrida, *Margins of Philosophy*, trans. Alan Bass (Chicago, IL: University of Chicago Press, 1982).

36. Roger T. Ames and David L. Hall, *Dao De Jing: A Philosophical Translation* (New York, NY: Ballantine Books, 2003).

37. Burton Watson, *Zhuangzi: Basic Writings* (New York: Columbia University Press, 2003).

38. It is interesting to note that even ideas about shadows themselves can be provocative. The nuanced meditation provided by the Japanese writer Jun'ichirō Tanizaki in his seminal book still retains its provocative power when compared to Western perceptions of gloom, Jun'ichirō Tanizaki, *In Praise of Shadows*, trans. Thomas J. Harper and Edward G. Seidensticker (London: Vintage, 2001 [1933]).

39. Brook Ziporyn, *The Penumbra Unbound: The Neo-Taoist Philosophy of Guo Xiang* (Albany, NY: SUNY Press, 2003).

40. The entanglements between the not-knowing and understanding are discussed in Eugene Thacker, *Starry Speculative Corpse* (New York, NY: Zer0 Books, 2015).

41. The shifting qualities of darkness are explored in Jacqueline Yallop, *What Darkness is and Why it Matters* (London: Icon Books, 2023).

42. Isaac Newton, *A New Theory of Light and Colours*, A Letter to the Royal Society (1671). Available at: https://www.earlymoderntexts.com/assets/pdfs/newton1671.pdf

43. Virginia Woolf, 'Monday 18 January [1915]', in *The Diary of Virginia Woolf, Volume 1: 1915–1919*, ed. Anne Olivier Bell (London: The Hogarth Press, 1977), p. 22.

44. See Rebecca Solnit, 'Woolf's Darkness: Embracing the Inexplicable', in *Men Explain Things to Me* (London: Granta, 2014), pp. 85–106.

45. Rebecca Solnit, *Hope in the Dark: Untold Histories Wild Possibilities* (Edinburgh: Canongate, 2005).

46. This situation and future scenarios that might play out has been provocatively explored in Naomi Oreskes and Erik M. Conway, *The Collapse of Western Civilization: A View from the Future* (New York, NY: Columbia University Press, 2014), and in the climate fiction genre, for example, Kim Stanley Robinson, *The Ministry for the Future* (London: Orbit Books, 2020).

47. For an incisive account of how our data drenched world is altering how our world is governed and how we (mis)understand it, see James Bridle, *New Dark Age: Technology and the End of the Future* (London: Verso, 2018).

48. See, respectively, Florence Williams, *The Nature Fix: Why Nature Makes Us Happier, Healthier, and More Creative* (New York, NY: W. W. Norton & Company, 2017), and Lucy Jones, *Losing Eden: Why Our Minds Need the Wild* (London: Allen Lane, 2020).

49. The phenomenon of offshoring is examined in John Urry, *Offshoring* (Cambridge: Polity, 2014).

50. For an example of how artificial light at night disrupts ecological rhythms, see Renee M. Borges, 'Dark Matters: Challenges of Nocturnal Communication Between Plants and Animals in Delivery of Pollination Services', in *Yale Journal of Biology and Medicine* 91:1 (March 2018), pp. 33–42. https://www.ncbi.nlm.nih.gov/pmc/articles/PMC5872639/

51. For instance, Arnaud Da Silva, Mihai Valcu, and Bart Kempenaers, 'Light pollution alters the phenology of dawn and dusk singing in common European songbirds', in *Philosophical Transactions of the Royal Society B* 370:1667 (May 2015), 20140126. https://doi.org/10.1098/rstb.2014.0126

52. For a nuanced inquiry into the subtle, ever-changing, and manifold sensory and metaphorical potency of twilight, see Peter Davidson, *The Last of the Light: About Twilight* (London: Reaktion, 2015).

Ecologies

53. This tendency is beautifully illustrated in the evocative examination of the Arctic where the tundra can initially appear barren as discussed by Barry Lopez, *Arctic Dreams: Imagination and Desire in a Northern Landscape* (New York, NY: Charles Scribner's Sons, 1986).

54. Pierantonio Cinzano, Fabio Falchi, and Christopher D. Elvidge, 'The first World Atlas of the artificial night sky brightness', in *Monthly Notices of the Royal Astronomical Society* 328:3 (December 2001), pp. 689–707. https://doi.org/10.1046/j.1365-8711.2001.04882.x

55. Fabio Falchi et al., 'The new world atlas of artificial night sky brightness', in *Science Advances* 2:6 (June 2016), e1600377. https://doi.org/10.1126/sciadv.1600377

56. Alejandro Sánchez de Miguel et al., 'First Estimation of Global Trends in Nocturnal Power Emissions Reveals Acceleration of Light Pollution', in *Remote Sensing* 13:16 (August 2021) 3311. https//doi.org/10.3390/rs13163311

57. See Charlotte Edmond, 'Global warming is heating up nights more quickly than days – with "profound" effects on wildlife', *Word Economic Forum* (7 October 2020). Available at: https://www.weforum.org/agenda/2020/10/global-warming-day-night-cloud-wildlife/

58. An early challenge to this view can be found in Michael P. Cohen, 'Blues in the Green: Ecocriticism Under Critique', in *Environmental History* 9:1 (January 2004), pp. 9–36.

59. As discussed by Ingemar Haag et al., 'Introduction' in *Perspectives on Ecocriticism: Local Beginnings, Global Echoes*, eds Ingemar Haag, Karin Molander Danielsson, Marie Öhman, and Thorste Päplow (Newcastle upon Tyne: Cambridge Scholars Publishing, 2019), pp. 1–8.

60. Timothy Morton, *Dark Ecology: For a Logic of Future Coexistence* (New York, NY: Columbia University Press, 2016).

61. For example, Kevin Gaston, Marcel E. Visser, and Franz Hölker (eds), 'The biological impacts of artificial light at night: From molecules to communities', in *Philosophical Transactions of the Royal Society B* 370:1667 (May 2015), 20140133. https://doi.org/10.1098/rstb.2014.0133

62. As discussed in Abraham Haim, David M. Scantlebury, and Abed E. Zubidat, 'The Loss of Ecosystem-services Emerging from Artificial Light at Night', in *Chronobiology International* 36:2 (2019), pp. 296–298. https://doi.org/10.1080/07420528.2018.1534122

63. For more information, see https://darksky.org

64. See Tory Shepherd, 'Picture imperfect', *The Guardian* (5 January 2023). Available at: https://www.theguardian.com/science/2023/jan/06/picture-imperfect-light-pollution-from-satellites-is-becoming-an-existential-threat-to-astronomy

65. Miroslav Kocifaj, Frantisek Kundracik, John C. Barentine, and Salvador Bará, 'The proliferation of space objects is a rapidly increasing source

of artificial night sky brightness', in *Monthly Notices of the Royal Astronomical Society: Letters* 504:1 (June 2021), pp. L40–L44. https://doi.org/10.1093/mnrasl/slab030

66. John C. Barentine et al., 'Aggregate effects of proliferating low-Earth-orbit objects and implications for astronomical data lost in the noise', in *Nature Astronomy* 7 (2023) pp. 252–258. https://doi.org/10.1038/s41550-023-01904-2

67. For an astonishing account of how other animals make sense of the world and how these sensescapes are under threat, see Ed Yong, 'Save the Quiet, Preserve the Dark', in *An Immense World: How Animal Senses Reveal the Hidden Realms Around Us* (London: The Bodley Head), pp. 335–355.

68. Jacques Rancière, 'The Distribution of the Sensible', in *The Politics of Aesthetics*, trans. Gabriel Rockhill (New York, NY: Continuum, 2009), pp. 7–46.

69. Kaitlyn M. Gaynor et al., 'The influence of human disturbance on wildlife nocturnality', in *Science* 360:6394 (2018), pp. 1232–1235. https://doi.org/10.1126/science.aar7121

70. Timothy M. Brown et al., 'Recommendations for daytime, evening, and nighttime indoor light exposure to best support physiology, sleep, and wakefulness in healthy adults', in *PLoS Biology*, 20:3 (2022), e3001571. https://doi.org/10.1371/journal.pbio.3001571

71. Filipa Rijo-Ferreira and Joseph S. Takahashi, 'Genomics of circadian rhythms in health and disease', in *Genome Medicine* 11:82 (2019), pp. 1–6. https://doi.org/10.1186/s13073-019-0704-0

72. YongMin Cho et al., 'Effects of Artificial Light at Night on Human Health: A Literature Review of Observational and Experimental Studies Applied to Exposure Assessment', in *Chronobiology International* 32:9 (2015), pp. 1294–1310. https://doi.org/10.3109/07420528.2015.1073158

73. To try and address such issues, Light Justice was established by Edward Bartholomew, Mark Loeffler, and Lya S. Osborn in 2022 as a forum for the practice of planning, designing, implementing, and investing in lighting for historically neglected communities through a process of stakeholder respect and engagement. For more info, see https://lightjustice.org

74. Steve M. Pawson and Martin K.-F. Bader, 'LED Lighting Increases the Ecological Impact of Light Pollution Irrespective of Color Temperature', in *Ecological Applications* 24:7 (2014), pp. 1561–1568. https://doi.org/10.1890/14-0468.1

75. There are exceptions, but they are small in number, for example, Paul Bogard, *Let There Be Night: Testimony on Behalf of the Dark* (Reno, NV: University of Nevada Press, 2008).

76. As discussed in Catherine Rich and Travis Longcore (eds), *Ecological Consequences of Artificial Night Lighting* (Washington, DC: Island Press, 2006).

77. Benjamin M. Van Doren et al., 'Intense Urban Lights Alter Bird Migration', in *Proceedings of the National Academy of Sciences* 114:42 (2017), pp. 11175–11180. https://doi.org/10.1073/pnas.1708574114

78. James J. Foster et al., J., Smolka, J., Nilsson, D., and Dacke, M. (2018) 'How animals follow the stars', in *Proceedings of the Royal Society B* 285:1871 (2018) 20172322. http://doi.org/10.1098/rspb.2017.2322

79. For example, Lin Meng et al., 'Artificial light at night: an underappreciated effect on phenology of deciduous woody plants', in *PNAS Nexus* 1:2 (May 2022), pgac046. https://doi.org/10.1093/pnasnexus/pgac046

Technologies

80. See Nick Dunn and Paul Cureton, 'Introduction: Futures, imagination and visions for cities', in *Future Cities: A Visual Guide* (London: Bloomsbury, 2020), pp. 1–28.

81. See, respectively, Nick Dunn and Paul Cureton, 'Technological Futures: Optimism, science fiction and infrastructural systems', ibid., pp. 80–110, and 'Global Futures: Challenges and opportunities for collective life', ibid., pp. 143–172.

82. As discussed in Nick Dunn and Paul Cureton, 'Frictionless Futures: The Vision of Smartness and the Occlusion of Alternatives', in *Architecture and the Smart City*, eds Sergio M. Figueiredo, Sukanya Krishnamurthy and Torsten Schroeder (London: Routledge, 2019), pp. 17–28.

83. Craig Koslofsky, *Evening's Empire: A History of the Night in Early Modern Europe* (Cambridge: Cambridge University Press, 2011).

84. For a compelling account of the development of artificial light, see Jane Brox, *Brilliant: The Evolution of Artificial Light* (New York, NY: Houghton Mifflin Harcourt, 2010).

85. For example, Chris Otter, *The Victorian Eye: A Political History of Light and Vision in Britain, 1800–1910* (Chicago, IL: University of Chicago Press, 2008).

86. As discussed in David E. Nye, *When the Lights Went Out: A History of Blackouts in America* (Cambridge, MA: The MIT Press, 2010).

87. As discussed by the insightful A. Roger Ekirch, *At Day's Close: A History of Nighttime* (London: Weidenfeld & Nicolson, 2005).

88. Thomas Carlyle, *Past and Present* (London: Chapman and Hall, 1843), p. 247.

89. This gloomy landscape and architecture of darkness is discussed further in Nick Dunn, 'Dark Futures: The Loss of Night in the Contemporary City?' in *Journal of Energy History / Revue d'Histoire de l'Énergie*, Special Issue: Light(s) and Darkness(es) / Lumière(s) et Obscurité(s), 1:2 (March 2019), pp. 1–27. http://energyhistory.eu/en/node/108

90. See Sandy Isenstadt, *Electric Light: An Architectural History* (Cambridge, MA: The MIT Press, 2019).

91. For example, Shawna M. Nadybal, Timothy W. Collins, and Sara E. Grineski, 'Light Pollution Inequities in the Continental United States: A Distributive Environmental Justice Analysis', in *Environmental Research* 189 (October 2020), 109959. https://doi.org/10.1016/j.envres.2020.109959

92. For example, Donna Goodman, *A History of the Future* (New York, NY: Monacelli Press, 2008).

93. This faith in technological optimism to solve all humanity's problems is examined in Douglas Murphy, *Last Futures: Nature, Technology and the End of Architecture* (London: Verso, 2016).

94. For example, Nicole Kalms, 'More Lighting Alone Does Not Create Safe Cities. Look at What Research with Young Women Tells Us', *The Conversation* (28 May 2019). Available at: https://theconversation.com/more-lighting-alone-does-not-create-safer-cities-look-at-what-research-with-young-women-tells-us-113359

95. Wolfganag Schivelbusch, *Disenchanted Night: The Industrialization of Light in the Nineteenth Century* (Berkeley, CA: University of California Press, 1988).

96. Joachim Schlör, *Nights in the Big City*, trans. Pierre Gottfried Imhof and Dafydd Rees Roberts (London: Reaktion Books, 1998).

97. Dietrich Neumann (ed.), *The Structure of Light: Richard Kelly and the Illumination of Modern Architecture* (New Haven, CT: Yale School of Architecture, 2010).

98. Edward Bartholomew, 2004. 'A Place for Darkness', in *Professional Lighting Design* (September/October 2004), pp. 38–41.

99. For example, Tim Edensor, 'The Gloomy City: Rethinking the Relation Between Light and Dark', in *Urban Studies* 52:3 (February 2015), pp. 422–438.

100. This is a topic I explore further in Nick Dunn, 'Dark Design: A New Framework for Advocacy and Creativity for the Nocturnal Commons', in *International Journal of Design in Society* 14:4 (2020), pp. 9–23.

101. DarkSky, 'Light pollution wastes energy and money and damages the climate' (17 October 2023). Available at: https://darksky.org/resources/what-is-light-pollution/effects/energy-climate/

102. For an authoritative account, see Bryan D. Palmer, *Cultures of Darkness: Night Travels in the Histories of Transgression* (New York, NY: Monthly Review Press, 2000).

103. For example, Oliver Dunnett, 'Contested Landscapes: The Moral Geographies of Light Pollution in Britain', in *Cultural Geographies* 22:4 (October 2015), pp. 619–636.

104. For example, Dave Haslam, *Life After Dark: A History of British Nightclubs and Music Venues* (London: Simon & Schuster, 2015).

105. This heterogeneity is discussed in Robert Williams, Robert. 2008. 'Nightspaces: Darkness, Deterritorialisation, and Social Control', in *Space and Culture* 11:4 (November 2008), pp. 514–532. https://doi.org/10.1177/1206331208320117

106. Nadia Drake, 'Our Nights are Getting Brighter, and Earth is Paying the Price', in *National Geographic* (3 April 2019). Available at: https://www.nationalgeographic.com/science/2019/04/nights-are-getting-brighter-earth-paying-the-price-light-pollution-dark-skies/

107. This line of inquiry has been the focus of much of the work of Taylor Stone, for example, 'Re-envisioning the Nocturnal Sublime: On the Ethics and Aesthetics of Nighttime Lighting', in *Topoi* 1:1 (2018). https://doi.org/10.1007/s11245-018-9562-4

108. See Tim Edensor, 'Dark Designs: Creating Shadow, Gloomy Spaces and Enchanting Light', in *Lighting Design in Shared Public Spaces*, ed. Shanti Sumartojo (New York, NY: Routledge), pp. 195–215.

109. DarkSky, 'France Adopts National Light Pollution Policy Among Most Progressive in the World' (9 January 2019). Available at: https://darksky. org/news/france-light-pollution-law-2018/

110. As discussed by Robert Shaw, *The Nocturnal City* (New York, NY: Routledge, 2018).

111. See, for example, Romain Sordello et al., 'A Plea for a Worldwide Development of Dark Infrastructure for Biodiversity – Practical Examples and Ways to Go Forward', in Landscape and Urban Planning 219 (March 2022), 104332. https://doi.org/10.1016/j. landurbplan.2021.104332

112. Thierry Cohen, *Villes Éteintes (Darkened Cities)* (2012). Available at: https://thierrycohen.com/pages/work/starlights.html

113. DarkSky, 'Five Principles for Responsible Outdoor Lighting'. Available at: https://darksky.org/resources/guides-and-how-tos/lighting-principles/

114. This idea is something I began to explore in Nick Dunn, 'Nocturnal Imaginaries: Rethinking and Redesigning the City After Dark', in *Ethnologies*, 44:1 (2023), pp. 107–128. https://doi. org/10.7202/1096059ar

115. See Jane Bennett, *Vibrant Matter: A Political Ecology of Things* (Durham, NC: Duke University Press, 2010).

116. The work being developed at the Dark Design Lab is developing new ways of capturing and communicating nonhuman activity after dark, for example, Rupert Griffiths and Nick Dunn, 'More-Than-Human Nights: Intersecting Lived Experience and Diurnal Rhythms in the Nocturnal City', in *ICNS Proceedings*, eds Manuel Garcia-Ruiz and Jordi Nofre (Lisbon: ISCTE, 2020), pp. 203–220.

117. For example, the work of Glowee. Available at: https://en.glowee.com

118. I have discussed this previously in Nick Dunn, 'Place After Dark: Urban Peripheries as Alternative Futures', in *The Routledge Handbook of Place*, eds Tim Edensor, Ares Kalandides, and Uma Kothari (London: Routledge, 2020), pp. 155–167.

Dark futures

119. Martin Sand, 'On "not having a future"', in *Futures* 107 (March 2019), pp. 98–106. https://doi.org/10.1016/j.futures.2019.01.002

120. Though later developed as a novel with Robert Silverberg and published in 1990, the original short story appeared as Isaac Asimov, 'Nightfall', in *Astounding Science-Fiction* ed. John W. Campbell (September 1941), pp. 9–34.

121. Here I refer the reader to the engaging and eloquent arguments put forward by Dani Robertson, *All Through The Night: Why Our Lives Depend on Dark Skies* (Manchester: HarperNorth, 2023).

122. The original photograph of the Earth taken on 7 December 1972 is available at: https://eol.jsc.nasa.gov/SearchPhotos/photo.pl?mission=AS17&roll=148&frame=22727

123. *Night Lights 2012 — The Black Marble* is an animated globe that depicts the city lights of the world as they appeared to the new Suomi NPP satellite which featured advanced light-resolving power than previous night-viewing satellites. Available at: https://earthobservatory.nasa.gov/images/79803/night-lights-2012-the-black-marble

124. This has been discussed by Sara B. Pritchard, 'The Trouble With Darkness: NASA's Suomi Satellite Images of Earth at Night', in *Environmental History* 22:2 (April 2017), pp. 312–330.

125. See Johan Eklöf, *The Darkness Manifesto: How Light Pollution Threatens the Ancient Rhythms of Life* trans. Elizabeth DeNoma (London: The Bodley Head, 2022).

126. For an excellent overview, see Jennifer M. Gidley, *The Future: A Very Short Introduction* (Oxford: Oxford University Press, 2017).

127. For example, Nick Montfort, *The Future* (Cambridge, MA: The MIT Press, 2017).

128. Johan Galtung, *Schooling, Education and the Future* 61 (Malmo: Department of Education and Psychology Research, Lund University, 1982).

129. Åke Bjerstedt, *Future Consciousness and the School* (Malmo: School of Education, University of Lund, 1982).

130. See Donna J. Haraway, *Staying with the Trouble: Making Kin in the Chthulucene* (Durham, NC: Duke University Press, 2016).

131. For example, Anna Tsing et al. (eds), *Arts of Living on a Damaged Planet: Ghosts and Monsters of the Anthropocene* (Minneapolis, MN: University of Minnesota, 2017).

Bestsellers from Zer0 Books include:

Poor but Sexy

Culture Clashes in Europe East and West
Agata Pyzik
How the East stayed East and the West stayed West.
Paperback:978-1-78099-394-2 ebook: 978-1-78099-395-9

An Anthropology of Nothing in Particular

Martin Demant Frederiksen
A journey into the social lives of meaninglessness.
Paperback: 978-1-78535-699-5 ebook: 978-1-78535-700-8

In the Dust of This Planet

Horror of Philosophy vol. 1
Eugene Thacker
In the first of a series of three books on the Horror of Philosophy,
In the Dust of This Planet offers the genre of horror as a way of
thinking about the unthinkable.
Paperback: 978-1-84694-676-9 ebook: 978-1-78099-010-1

The End of Oulipo?

An Attempt to Exhaust a Movement
Lauren Elkin, Veronica Esposito
Paperback: 978-1-78099-655-4 ebook: 978-1-78099-656-1

Capitalist Realism

Is There No Alternative?
Mark Fisher
An analysis of the ways in which capitalism has presented itself
as the only realistic political-economic system.
Paperback: 978-1-84694-317-1 ebook: 978-1-78099-734-6

Rebel Rebel

Chris O'Leary
David Bowie: every single song. Everything you want to know,
everything you didn't know.
Paperback: 978-1-78099-244-0 ebook: 978-1-78099-713-1

Cartographies of the Absolute

Alberto Toscano, Jeff Kinkle
An aesthetics of the economy for the twenty-first century.
Paperback: 978-1-78099-275-4 ebook: 978-1-78279-973-3

Malign Velocities

Accelerationism and Capitalism
Benjamin Noys
Long-listed for the Bread and Roses Prize 2015, *Malign Velocities*
argues against the need for speed, tracking acceleration
as the symptom of the ongoing crises of capitalism.
Paperback: 978-1-78279-300-7 ebook: 978-1-78279-299-4

Babbling Corpse

Vaporwave and the Commodification of Ghosts
Grafton Tanner
Paperback: 978-1-78279-759-3 ebook: 978-1-78279-760-9

New Work New Culture

Work we want and a culture that strengthens us
Frithjof Bergmann
A serious alternative for humankind and the planet.
Paperback: 978-1-78904-064-7 ebook: 978-1-78904-065-4

Romeo and Juliet in Palestine

Teaching Under Occupation
Tom Sperlinger
Life in the West Bank, the nature of pedagogy, and the role of a
university under occupation.
Paperback: 978-1-78279-637-4 ebook: 978-1-78279-636-7

Color, Facture, Art and Design

Iona Singh
This materialist definition of fine art develops guidelines for
architecture, design, cultural studies, and ultimately, social
change.
Paperback: 978-1-78099-629-5 ebook: 978-1-78099-630-1

Sweetening the Pill

or How We Got Hooked on Hormonal Birth Control
Holly Grigg-Spall
Has contraception liberated or oppressed women?
Sweetening the Pill breaks the silence on the dark side of hormonal contraception.
Paperback: 978-1-78099-607-3 ebook: 978-1-78099-608-0

Why Are We the Good Guys?

Reclaiming Your Mind from the Delusions of Propaganda
David Cromwell
A provocative challenge to the standard ideology that Western power is a benevolent force in the world.
Paperback: 978-1-78099-365-2 ebook: 978-1-78099-366-9

The Writing on the Wall

On the Decomposition of Capitalism and its Critics
Anselm Jappe, Alastair Hemmens
A new approach to the meaning of social emancipation.
Paperback: 978-1-78535-581-3 ebook: 978-1-78535-582-0

Neglected or Misunderstood

The Radical Feminism of Shulamith Firestone
Victoria Margree
An interrogation of issues surrounding gender, biology, sexuality, work, and technology, and the ways in which our imaginations continue to be in thrall to ideologies of maternity and the nuclear family.
Paperback: 978-1-78535-539-4 ebook: 978-1-78535-540-0

**How to Dismantle the NHS in 10 Easy Steps
(Second Edition)**
Youssef El-Gingihy
The story of how your NHS was sold off and why you will have
to buy private health insurance soon. A new expanded second
edition with chapters on junior doctors' strikes and government
blueprints for US-style healthcare.
Paperback: 978-1-78904-178-1 ebook: 978-1-78904-179-8

Digesting Recipes

The Art of Culinary Notation
Susannah Worth
A recipe is an instruction, the imperative tone of the expert, but
this constraint can offer its own kind of potential. A recipe need
not be a domestic trap but might instead offer escape—
something to fantasise about or aspire to.
Paperback: 978-1-78279-860-6 ebook: 978-1-78279-859-0

Most titles are published in paperback and as an ebook.
Paperbacks are available in traditional bookshops. Both print and
ebook formats are available online.
Follow us at:
https://www.facebook.com/ZeroBooks
https://twitter.com/Zer0Books
https://www.instagram.com/zero.books

You Tube

For video content, author interviews, and more, please subscribe to our YouTube channel:

zer0repeater

Follow us on social media for book news, promotions, and more:

Facebook: ZeroBooks

Instagram: @zero.books

X: @Zer0Books

Tik Tok: @zer0repeater

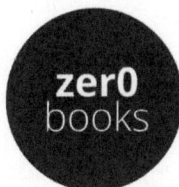

zer0
books